CAPE COD COMPANION

The History and Mystery of
Old Cape Cod

CAPE COD COMPANION

The History and Mystery of Old Cape Cod

Jack Sheedy
Jim Coogan

Harvest Home Books
East Dennis, Massachusetts

In cooperation with
The Barnstable Patriot
Hyannis, Massachusetts

CAPE COD COMPANION

First Printing – August 1999
Second Printing – April 2000
Third Printing – August 2001

Published by
Harvest Home Books, P.O. Box 1181
East Dennis, Massachusetts 02641

In cooperation with
The Barnstable Patriot, P.O. Box 1208
Hyannis, Massachusetts 02601

ISBN 0-9672596-0-6

Cover design and text layout by Kristen vonHentschel

Printed in the United States of America

Additional copies of Cape Cod Companion may be
obtained by contacting Harvest Home Books or *The
Barnstable Patriot* at the addresses above.

Essays contained in Cape Cod Companion were
initially published in the 1989-1991 and 1994-2000
issues of *The Barnstable Patriot*'s magazine
supplement *Summerscape*.

TABLE OF CONTENTS

TABLE OF CONTENTS Cont...

INTRODUCTION

In June of 1983, Mrs. Barbara Haskins Williams, the owner of *The Barnstable Patriot*, decided to celebrate the 153rd anniversary of the newspaper by publishing a summer supplement entitled *Summerscape*. The first issue appropriately focused on seasons past with a rich trove of *Patriot* history blended with the Cape's fame as a summer holiday destination.

Upon our arrival in 1994 we set about to zestfully expand the effort to reach more Cape Codders and visitors with intriguing stories which unearth the peninsula's wonderful history from pre-Colonial times forward. The Cape and her people, the land, the sea and maritime history, tales of farming and industry, the revolution and wars. The tapestry of this land, and especially the people, is simply incredible.

Each June we bring forth another issue and almost every January the New England Press Association smiles on our efforts with an award for editorial excellence. We publish, I dare say, the only summer reading not crammed with information on vanilla ice cream, miniature golf or hard-body beaches.

Thanks go to Jack and Jim, obviously, but their passion for history, our collective history, is matched and occasionally tempered by *The Patriot*'s skillful editor David Still. Kristen vonHentschel's design work, evident here and in the paper, speaks for her precision and eye and to our good fortune.

Wander these pages to enjoy and to marvel.

Toni and Rob Sennott
July, 1999
Hyannis, Cape Cod, MA

FOREWORD

Every town on Cape Cod has its own unique history, its own stories both great and small which, when gathered up together, represent the whole. From their pioneer settlers have grown fifteen towns on this one peninsula from Bourne to Provincetown, each town weaving its own part of the tapestry that we today call Cape Cod.

Before the arrival of the Europeans there were, of course, the Native Indians who themselves arrived here between 5,000 and 10,000 years ago after the last ice age. After the arrival of the European explorers during the early years of the seventeenth century the Indians found themselves in a state of decline. Sadly, one-sided land agreements and epidemics wiping out entire tribes during the eighteenth century led to their ultimate demise. Upon former Indian lands the rugged settlers and descendants of settlers carved out their humble existence.

During the nineteenth century the bogs of the Cape ripened with cranberries, vats whitened with salt from the sea, fish were harvested from the waves of the Atlantic and whales were hunted in the Pacific. Fearless sea captains opened up trade routes to foreign ports around the globe, their crafts and crews setting speed records and making Cape Cod a player in the world market. Cape women even got into the act, sailing with their seafaring husbands and even stepping in when they fell ill or died during the course of a voyage.

With the sea came shipwrecks. The treacherous coastline around this sandy peninsula rendered Cape Cod a graveyard for hundreds and hundreds of wrecked vessels and their lost crews. Aiding these mariners were thirteen lifesaving stations lining the Lower Cape coastline, their brave crews walking the beaches each night on watch for disasters. "You must go out!" was the rule, and out they went, launching their surfboats into the icy seas to land

9

shipwreck survivors.

Also lining the coastline were stoic lighthouses, their solitary beams slicing through the darkness and the fog and the rain as beacons of hope to those sailing in the pitch offshore. Many of these majestic guardians are with us still today, lifelines reaching from the proud nineteenth century world of our ancestors to our own world racing toward the twenty-first century.

Cape Codders have fought in all of our country's wars ... even before there was a country to fight for. A Barnstable native by the name of James Otis, Jr. is perhaps the single person who lit the very flame of freedom that continued to burn into the Declaration of Independence and, ultimately, the Revolutionary War. Fanning this flame was Otis' sister Mercy who penned political satire meant to further promote the patriots' cause. Meanwhile, the town of Falmouth was bombarded by the British Navy during the Revolutionary War as well as during the War of 1812. Orleans was also shelled by the British, in 1814, and also by the Germans, in 1918, marking the only attack against American soil during World War I.

The Cape has been the summer home to a number of U.S. Presidents, including Grover Cleveland who was both the twenty-second and twenty-fourth president. Orleans was home to the French Cable Company; Wellfleet was home to the Marconi wireless station – both institutions connecting the United States to Europe and the rest of the world.

The forest of Barnstable was home to an eighteenth century witch named Liza Tower Hill. The moors of Eastham were home to the Lower Cape witch Goody Hallett. And the waters around this peninsula were home to a legion of sea serpents.

These stories, provided in this collection as essays, all appeared as original articles in *The Barnstable Patriot's* magazine supplement *Summerscape*. I have had the pleasure of contributing to this supplement for the past eleven years, and serving as managing editor for the past two. As I look back at the past issues in preparing this collection, I smile at our efforts and at the partnerships and friendships that have been forged over those years.

My initial involvement with *Summerscape* was through then

publisher Barbara Williams who was very supportive of my work during those early years. Equally supportive have been Rob and Toni Sennott who took over the reins as publishers in 1994 and who, along with editor David Still II and graphic designer Kristen vonHentschel, have expanded *Summerscape* into the award-winning piece that it is today. Rob, Toni and David have given me the freedom to be creative, a rarity in publishing these days, and for this I am very grateful. And Kristen, who not only serves as graphic designer for *The Patriot* and *Summerscape* but also designed the cover and text layout for this collection, is always a pleasure to work with ... even when deadline is looming and I have "just a couple more changes to the text."

Summerscape received a huge "shot in the arm" in 1995. That was the year Jim Coogan joined the writing staff. A history teacher at Dennis-Yarmouth Regional High School for twenty-seven years and a popular lecturer on Cape Cod history, Jim's involvement with *Summerscape* took the magazine to a whole new level. He is a treasure trove of Cape Cod history, able to speak intelligently on nearly any subject from the Canal to the tip of the Cape. Over these past five years I have deeply enjoyed his many insightful articles and am looking forward to those to come in future issues of *Summerscape*.

Jim and I recently learned that we share more than our common interest in Cape Cod. It turns out that our ancestors hailed from the same county in Ireland – Monaghan. As Jim put it, "They probably broke sod and raised pints together." The tradition continues, as I am proud to consider Jim not only my colleague and co-author, but also my friend.

I would be amiss not to thank my wife, Adriana, for her support and guidance throughout these past eleven years, and especially these past months as I've worked toward preparing this collection for publication. She often reviews and critiques my work prior to publication, and I am very thankful for that! Her watchful eyes have caught many a typo and her thoughtful suggestions have improved many an article.

This project has been more than three years in the making. I clearly remember a spring day back in 1996 when Rob Sennott and I first kicked around the idea of publishing a collection of *Summerscape* articles in book form. There have been many detours over these past three years, but none of us ever lost sight of the finish line. Now, as I type these final sentences and words I breathe a sigh of relief that the idea we hatched years ago is finally reaching fruition. It has been a long journey, but I would not have had it any other way. Over these past three years *Cape Cod Companion* has evolved into something of which we can all be proud.

The articles that comprise the text of this collection have appeared in *Summerscapes* from 1989 to 1999, and one article that did not appear in the 1999 issue due to space considerations is slated to run in the 2000 issue of the supplement. In that sense, this collection represents a dozen years of work.

As we prepare to leave not only this century, but also this millennium for the next, I hope you will enjoy journeying with us for this look back at Cape Cod of centuries past.

Ten thousand stories comprise Cape Cod ... ten thousand and ten thousand more. In this volume we have compiled a smattering of those thousands of stories, some familiar and some not so familiar, some fact and some legend, all pieces that represent the whole of this place called Cape Cod.

Jack Sheedy, Editor
July, 1999
East Dennis, MA

Chapter
1

Natives, Norsemen
& a New World

Cape Cod was formed more than ten thousand years ago during a glacial epoch, it was discovered more than five thousand years ago by Native Indians, and rediscovered four hundred years ago by European explorers.

Indian dominance over these outer lands and outer shores was never questioned until the handful of years following the arrival of the Pilgrims in 1620. Within time, as more white settlers arrived on this narrow peninsula, the Native Indians began to feel the squeeze. Though they were able to stave off a potential Norse conquest during the eleventh century, they had no defense against the steady flow of Europeans to arrive during the seventeenth century. In the end, the Indians were virtually wiped out during the eighteenth century

Cape Cod Geology

Many motorists drive the Mid-Cape highway from Sandwich to
Orleans and never realize that they are moving along an ancient
geological debris field that came with the last ice age almost 10,000
years ago.

Present day Cape Cod is a product of wind, water and glacial
action. But it is the latter and oldest force that represents the
greatest influence on the shape of the unique peninsula that we
live on. There are no outcroppings of solid rock here as can be
found in other parts of the Northeast. The bedrock of granite that
is the underpinning of Cape Cod, and indeed all of New England,
lies far beneath the clay, silt, and sand that make up what locals
euphemistically call "soil."

In the opinion of climatologists, at some point in the earth's more
recent history there was a temperature change and the earth
became colder. The cold period lasted for hundreds, perhaps
thousands of years. The effect of the cooling was a corresponding
lowering of the sea levels and the expansion of great sheets of ice
or superglaciers that began their inexorable movement southward.
At one point in the last great ice age, it is estimated that almost one
third of the Northern Hemisphere of the globe was encased in ice.
As would be the case if one were to pile scoops upon scoops of ice
cream on a plate, eventually, the increasing weight of the frozen
mass would force the outer edges to move away from the center.
This was the effect of layers upon layers of snow massing in the
high latitudes and the subsequent southern movement of the ice
sheets that carried all before it.

As the great superglaciers began to slowly gouge the landscape
like a plow, the facing edge of the ice moved tons of boulders and
particles of soil known as till. In the first great wave of ice, some
twenty to twenty-five thousand years ago, the moraine, or final
ridge of debris, was deposited in the present locations of Martha's
Vineyard and Nantucket. Because it represents the furthest movement south, this ridge of land is referred to as a terminal moraine.

A second renewal of a southern ice sheet, which arrived little
more than 10,000 years ago, stopped in the vicinity of the northern

edge of what is now Cape Cod. This is a recessional moraine. In both eras, the melting ice created outwash channels that moved both water and till to the south, creating ancient rivers whose forgotten channels can be found today by soundings in Nantucket Sound and to the south of both islands.

With the warming temperatures, more ice melted and the sea levels rose, working on the soft edges of the exposed land. Wind and wave action ground the glacial debris into sand, which then migrated and collected along the coast. Most of Provincetown, Barnstable's Sandy Neck, and all of Monomoy Island are perhaps the best examples of sand migration deposited by long shore currents. On the ground that remained above sea level, the outwash channels became the familiar rivers that are part of the present landscape. It is interesting to note that most all of these rivers, like their ancient predecessors, flow in a southerly direction.

When the face of the glacier began to break up as the earth warmed, huge singular blocks of ice were deposited on the moraine. These eventually melted, forming most of the round glacial "kettle ponds" that are prevalent on Cape Cod. On the southern plains of both Cape Cod and the Islands, spring fed ponds fill depressions left from the location of large glacial ice chunks. There are more than three hundred and fifty of them.

What few large boulders there are on both the Cape and Islands are found on the northern edges of both landmasses. Here, on the north edge are the rough highlands of Cape Cod. The land in Barnstable village, for example, is much higher and rockier than is the land at Hyannis, Cotuit and Centerville. Geological borings confirm that the lighter materials under the surface of the land are situated on the southern slope of both the Cape and Islands and are closer to sea level. The effect of this geology meant that farming tended to be a bit easier on the southern edges of both Cape Cod and the Islands because the land was more level with fewer obstructions to plowing. A close look at the land will also reveal fewer stone walls on the south coastal plains.

None of this scientific geology was available to native people on Cape Cod. In their far more colorful explanation of how the physical landscape of the peninsula came to be, it was the result of a giant Indian, Maushop, who shaped the land. Maushop was so large that when he slept he supported his head on the dunes of Provincetown and his feet scraped the southeast coast of Falmouth. While asleep, the mosquitoes would annoy Maushop and as he tossed and turned, his elbows and knees gouged out the many ponds and valleys of Cape Cod. Another tale tells of a giant fish that desired a shortcut from Nantucket Sound to Cape Cod Bay. At the urging of the Indians, this giant fish swam inland as far as Santuit Pond, creating the river that runs to the sea, and resting forever in the quiet waters of legend.

The lasting impact of the great ice age can be visibly tracked today by siting the line of water towers that parallel the upland ridges along the Mid-Cape highway. These high points mark the greatest extent of the debris field that was deposited long ago. The constant winds that blow across the peninsula, coupled with the incessant wave action along the coastline, put the finishing touches on the formation of Cape Cod.

But these changes are by no means final, as any resident would readily agree. Cape Cod and the Islands are still a work in progress as far as the natural forces of wind and water are concerned. Given enough time, the peninsula and its island cousins to the south will eventually succumb to these forces and the cycle will have come full circle.

Norse Discovery of Vinland

Once in a while we find ourselves confronted with a piece of folklore that may actually be a true piece of history. So it is with the notion that Viking explorers discovered and later settled on Cape Cod one thousand years ago.

Norse expeditions did venture southwestward of Iceland between the years 980 and 1005 AD, but just how far southwestward did they travel and exactly where did they establish their temporary settlement? Some historians believe the location is none other than the narrow peninsula of Cape Cod.

Imagine the Cape one millennium ago, a vast wilderness of forests, untamed, brimming with animals and vegetation. Pockets of Indians inhabited this land, yet one could probably walk for days without happening upon one. It was, perhaps, an Eden with lush woodlands, cascading dunes, and waves crashing upon lonely beaches for mile after unbroken mile. The summers were warm but not oppressive, the autumns were cool and colorful, and the winters were relatively mild with an occasional storm. It seemed the perfect place for a group of voyagers from more northern and colder climes to settle.

According to the Norse sagas handed down over the ages, the land that we today call Cape Cod was discovered in 989 AD by a Viking explorer named Bjarni Herjulfsson. He left Iceland and neighboring Greenland, passing three landmasses along his journey. The first is believed to be Newfoundland. Herjulfsson continued onward into unexplored seas, apparently not fearing that his vessel would fall off the end of the earth or else be devoured by some gigantic sea serpent lurking just outside the reaches of the then known world.

He next passed a second landmass considered to be Nova Scotia. Southwestward, he arrived at a third piece of land, believed to be Cape Cod. For reasons unknown he decided not to make landfall. Upon his return to Iceland he told of his journey and of the new worlds he discovered along the way. Amongst those who would later hear the tales was Leif Erikson, son of Erik the Red, who was only eleven years old when Herjulfsson made his historic journey.

For more than a decade no one ventured southwestward along Herjulfsson's path. The Norse, it seemed, were content with Iceland and Greenland despite the stories of warmer lands resting just beyond the horizon. The greatest discovery of any era - the discovery of a New World - was nearly overlooked, existing only within the sagas spoken at the village gatherings to keep the memories alive.

But, about the year 1000 AD, Leif Erikson suddenly became interested in the idea of seeking out and exploring this New World. Recently converted to Christianity, he decided it was his mission to venture to new lands such as Greenland and those that rested to the west to spread his newfound religion. He obtained a vessel and a crew of thirty-five men from Herjulfsson, a number of the men having sailed to the new lands fourteen years before, and departed Iceland for whatever rested ahead.

After stopping at Greenland to convert the population there, Leif followed Herjulfsson's earlier path taking him past Newfoundland, which he named Helluland for the mountains of ice and snow, and Nova Scotia, which he named Markland for its rich forests of trees. After many days upon open water he arrived at Cape Cod in September.

Into Nantucket Sound he sailed. The saga tells that Leif and his crew first landed at an island resting just north of another landmass, with a cape off to the north. With that description, historians surveyed the northeast coast for such a location. One locale seems to fit the scenario - Great Point off the island of Nantucket. Here they went ashore for a short period and noted that the dew in the grass tasted sweet, like honey.

With their eyes on the cape lying to the north, they climbed back onto their ship and sailed across the sound. The saga tells that they came to a river that flows down from a lake. Bass River is such a river that lies just northwest of Great Point. At low tide, the ship became grounded at the mouth of the river, but when the tide turned the ship was lifted free and up the river the Vikings ventured.

Erikson navigated his vessel the length of Bass River, some five miles into the heart of Cape Cod, to Follins Pond, which today separates Dennis and Yarmouth. Here he anchored, went ashore and built shelter.

Folklore tells that Leif sent two Gaelic members of his crew, a woman named Haekia and a man named Haki, both fleet of foot, to explore the land. They returned proclaiming that the territories through which they traveled were rich with vegetation, and in their arms they carried the proof. Leif named his newly explored land Vinland for the grapevines that grew here at the time in such abundant fashion.

The Norse expedition spent the winter at the settlement on Follins Pond. Come spring, they loaded up their vessel with the fruits of the Cape and departed for Greenland and Iceland beyond. It is believed that Leif Erikson never again returned to his Vinland.

Throughout the winter of his return, tales of Leif Erikson's

voyage to Vinland were retold again and again amongst the
icebound Greenlanders. Come spring of the following year, Leif's
brother Thorwald wished to try his luck in the New World.

Thorwald wanted Leif to journey with him, but he refused. Their
father recently died and Leif, being the eldest son, now took his
place as master of the Great Hall at Brattahlid, Greenland. He lent
Thorwald his ship to sail to Vinland where he could stay in the
settlement he and his men built the year before.

Arriving at Leif's camp on Follins Pond, the group was immediately struck by misfortune. The weather was horrible, the fish were
not biting and hunting was even less fruitful. The band of settlers
began to discount the wonderful stories of Vinland that they heard
all the previous winter.

Facing starvation in this seemingly Eden-like environment, one
member of the group named Thornhall the Hunter set off alone to
the shoreline and prayed for Thor to bless them with a bounty.
Very soon a whale was sighted. The men set after it in a boat and
were successful in capturing and killing the whale. They dragged
it ashore and ate of its blubber, but when these good Christians
realized that Thornhall appealed to the god Thor for their salvation
they all became ill. To rid themselves of the sickness, they hauled
the whale carcass out to sea and then rowed back to land to pray
for forgiveness. Afterwards, the stormy weather abated, and fish
and game stocks grew plentiful.

After a time Thorwald decided to explore the peninsula. He and
his crew sailed around Monomoy Island and up the backside of
the Cape to Provincetown where the ship suffered a damaged keel
on the shoals. Repairs were made, the ship was re-keeled, and
Thorwald had the old keel timbers erected at the beach there,
naming the land "Keelness."

With the ship repaired, they rounded the tip and entered Cape
Cod Bay, sailing to what is now Bass Hole. Here they discovered a
small band of Indians on the beach. Fearing that the Indians would
alert more of their tribe to the Viking's presence, Thorwald had the
Indians killed. But one Indian escaped the massacre and ran off to
warn the tribe.

Soon Thorwald and his men were attacked by a much larger

group of natives, or as the Norse called them, Skraellings. Thorwald took an arrow in the chest and fell to the sand, mortally wounded. The Norsemen were successful in defending themselves against the Skraellings, and chased them off. As Thorwald lay dying, he asked that he be buried on the beach and, being Christian, asked that the men erect a cross at the head and foot of his grave. The men called the place where Thorwald was buried "Crossness," loosely translated as Cape of Crosses.

Thorwald's expedition remained on Vinland for two years before departing for Greenland. Upon their return, Leif's other brother, Thorstein, announced he would sail for Vinland to retrieve Thorwald's body and return it to Greenland. Thorstein was married to Gudrid, the widow of Thorir. Gudrid and Thorir were rescued at sea years earlier by Leif Erikson upon his return trip from Vinland.

Together, Thorstein and Gudrid set off for Vinland to bring back Thorwald's body, but after months at sea became hopelessly lost. Somehow they made it back to Greenland where Thorstein later died of an epidemic that swept through the village where they landed.

Gudrid was once again a widow, but not for long. Thorfinn Karlsefni, from Norway, arrived at Greenland to visit with Leif. There he met Gudrid and very soon the two were married. Shortly thereafter, Thorfinn decided he would like to start a settlement in the New World.

So, in the year 1007 AD, with three ships, 165 men and women, and as much livestock as the ships could carry, he set off across the ocean toward Vinland. Thus began the first attempted colonization of the Americas.

Along with Thorfinn and his wife Gudrid sailed Leif's half-sister Freydis and her husband. They arrived in summer and instantly succeeded in taming the land to their purposes. They were able to hunt and fish and occasionally capture a whale. During the following year the Norsemen made contact with the native Skraellings. A peaceful meeting transpired. Trade between the two groups commenced.

Later that year, Gudrid gave birth to a son. Named Snorri, he is considered the first European child to be born in the New World. Shortly afterwards the Skraellings returned to barter, but the meeting ended in disaster. A Skraelling was accused of stealing one of the Vikings' weapons, and was subsequently killed. The remaining Indians fled the camp.

Skraellings returned later by canoe in greater numbers. Thorfinn realized they were not coming for trade, but rather for revenge. A battle ensued and, as the sagas relate, the frightened Norse were saved by the heroics of Freydis who picked up a sword from a dead Viking laying nearby and did battle with a number of Skraellings, inspiring the other Norse to rally to victory.

Despite their victory over the Skraellings, Thorfinn could sense that his dream of a Vinland settlement was not to be. Fear of attack became an everyday risk. And now their own society was beginning to break down. Men grossly outnumbered the women, a cause for great concern amongst those without a partner. After nearly four years, the group loaded up their vessels, abandoned their settlement and departed for Greenland.

The very next year, around 1011 AD, talk began once again of a Vinland settlement. Two Icelandic brothers, Helgi and Finnborgi, heard the stories of a warmer land resting to the southwest and decided to give it a try. Meanwhile, Freydis learned of Helgi and Finnborgi's plan. She borrowed Leif's vessel and joined the expedition.

Upon their arrival the two groups instantly began to distrust one another and ultimately settled in different areas. One evening, Freydis awoke her husband with claims that she visited the other camp to negotiate a trade agreement with the two brothers, but instead they mistreated her. The men of Freydis' camp raided the other camp where they killed Helgi and Finnborgi and all the rest of the men in their sleep. With an axe, Freydis butchered the camp's five women.

That next spring, Freydis decided that she had her fill of the New World. She ordered the two ships loaded with the gifts of the land and off they sailed back to Greenland. Thus ends the saga of the Eden-like Vinland.

The Norse never conquered this land. They tried many times.

Some believe there is evidence of their presence from Nova Scotia to Cape Cod where it is thought they first stepped foot upon the New World. Rune stones pointing to their presence in North America were unearthed in many places, including at Bourne where one was discovered in 1658. The scratchings on the Bourne stone apparently translate as "Jesus amply provides for us here and in heaven," yet that translation and the origin of the scratches on the stone were questioned over the years.

Perhaps it was an old Viking foundation that was unearthed in Provincetown in the mid-1800s. Perhaps it was a Viking shoring that was discovered in 1952 on the edges of Follins Pond, and Viking mooring holes discovered in the large boulders on the banks of Bass River. Yet, if Leif Erikson did arrive at North America a thousand years ago there were hundreds of rivers from Florida to Nova Scotia up which he could have sailed to make his settlement. Saga evidence seems to favor Cape Cod as its latitude matches the vague latitudinal inferences in the sagas.

We may never know if Vikings landed at Cape Cod. Physical evidence is certainly lacking. All that remain are the tales of Bjarni Herjulfsson's discovery of the peninsula, Leif Erikson's landing and initial settlement, Thorwald's battle with the Skraellings and Thorfinn's attempted colonization. Until there is unearthed a rune stone bearing the inscription "Leif Erikson was here, 1000 AD" we may never know for sure.

The Hills of Truro

It is ironic that today's least populated town on Cape Cod was very nearly the spot selected by the *Mayflower* Pilgrims to become their new Plymouth upon arrival in the fall of 1620.

Landing at the tip of the Cape in November, a group of sixteen or so Pilgrims, among them William Bradford and Myles Standish, set off on foot to explore the lands lying to the south in search of food, water and possibly a home. Three expeditions were conducted, the first two leading into what is today Truro, and the third expedition winding up in Eastham where the small band of Pilgrims first met up with the Native Indians at what is now called First Encounter

This bas relief monument depicts the Pilgrims signing the Mayflower Compact while at Provincetown Harbor in 1620. (J. Sheedy photo)

Beach. There would be many such encounters to follow.

Truro is a land consisting of many magnificent hills and sweeping valleys with moors and marshlands and woodlands in between. The Tudoresque airs of Vaughan Williams' *Fantasia on a Theme by Thomas Tallis* come to mind as one travels through this Truro countryside that more nearly resembles the rolling fields and hills of England than the dunes and pitch pines of Cape Cod. These hills marked the town's history over the centuries during her best and worst of times.

Truro's hills are legendary, and just as legendary are their names: the Hill of Churches, the Hill of Storms, Corn Hill, Pilgrim Heights and the Clay Pounds of the Highlands. The entire east coast of Truro facing the Atlantic seems as if one continuous cliff, in some places rising more than one hundred feet above the beach and the ocean beyond. Each hill has its own character and its own history. Each hill holds its own chapter in the book of Cape Cod.

At Pilgrim Heights in North Truro is where the whole story begins. In November of that memorable year of 1620, the Pilgrims tasted their first fresh water in the New World at what is now referred to as Pilgrim Spring. What a grand discovery that must have been. Myles Standish, in his journal entries that

The Congregational Church, also known as the "Bell" Church, sits atop Truro's Hill of Churches surrounded by her cemetery. (J. Sheedy photo)

survived via the Pilgrim chronicle *Mourt's Relation*, indicated that at first a number of the Pilgrims were skeptical about drinking from the spring. You can just picture the gruff Standish's reply to the skeptics, probably something like, "Well, we're not about to sail all the way back to England every time you folks desire a glass of water!" Eventually, all the Pilgrims drank of the spring and found the water to be of good quality. The marked location of Pilgrim Spring is, of course, a contemporary historian's best guess as to where the spring was located. Pilgrim Heights itself is a splendid overlook offering wonderful views of the valleys and marshes below.

Corn Hill, also marked by a plaque, is located near Cape Cod Bay just northwest of Truro Center. It was here where the Pilgrims discovered a cache of Indian corn buried in grass woven baskets. The kernels from this discovery, as well as a number of return trips to the same deserted Indian village, formed the seeds of the Pilgrim's first harvest. Yes, that's right, during their very first days in the New World the Pilgrims, who referred to themselves as "Saints," stole the Native Indians' corn! But that wasn't all they stole. The Pilgrims also came across Indian graves and home sites, taking whatever they felt would help them to survive. Who can truly blame them, in a strange land with winter approaching.

At one site during their initial visit they found an iron kettle that they filled with corn and carried away with them. The discovery of the kettle, and the discovery of a grave containing a sailor, are interesting finds pointing to earlier European contact with the Indians. Returning north with the kettle and their pockets full of corn, the band of Pilgrims encamped on the shores of a Truro pond, the area now referred to as Pond Village. Fearing Indian retaliation, they sank the kettle in the pond so not to be found. A year or two later the Pilgrims, found out and feeling guilty about their earlier crime, compensated the Indians for the corn they stole.

The settlement of Truro, originally called Pamet or Payomet by the Native Indians, happened well after many other towns on Cape. With the settlement of Nauset, later Eastham, by Thomas Prence and other "Pilgrims" is 1644, the lands to the north were included under the terms of the land grant. Those lands today make up the towns of Wellfleet, Truro and Provincetown. A group of Eastham folk going by the name of the Pamet Proprietors began negotiating with the Indians of the area in 1689, and by 1694 the notion of a municipality was formed under the name of Pamet. In 1705, the name of the area was changed to Dangerfield and received municipal privileges. Four years later, in 1709, Dangerfield was incorporated as the town of Truro, named after the English town because the hills and moors resembled those of the Cornish countryside of the settlers' native land.

At that time, the Province Lands were also part of Truro, although the people of Truro really wanted nothing to do with the land to the north where law and order were nonexistent. These Province Lands broke away in 1714 to become its own town, Provincetown. Both towns then got down to the business of fishing and whaling. By 1758, Truro's first whaling vessel, aptly named *Whale*, was working the grounds off Greenland.

Around 1710, a meeting house was built at the Hill of Storms about midway between what is today Truro center and North

Truro. Prior to the building of Highland Lighthouse in 1797, this
church, known as the North Cemetery Church, served not only as
a source of inspiration but also as a landmark for mariners attempting to dodge the treacherous shoals and bars offshore.

Methodists arrived at Truro during the early 1790s and in 1794
built their meeting house, the first Methodist meeting house on
Cape Cod and only the second such meeting house in all of New
England. In 1826, the Methodists rebuilt their church to the south
at what is known as the Hill of Churches. Over the years the
location of the Hill of Storms became inconvenient to the populations now settling to the south where Pamet Harbor was situated
along with its spin-off businesses. Throughout the 1820s and 1830s
the North Church lost members and with the building of a Union
Church in 1840, the North Church on the Hill of Storms was torn
down during that same year. The cemetery, containing the oldest
gravestones in town, one dating to 1712, is all that remains of the
north parish of Truro.

Meanwhile, religion was in full swing at the Hill of Churches in
Truro Center. One year after the Methodists built their meeting
house on the hill, the Congregationalists followed suit with their
own church. This church still stands near the crest of the hill, in its
steeple is a bell fashioned by Paul Revere's son and in its windows
are glass blown by Sandwich Glassworks. Her cemetery is nearly
as beautiful as the church building itself. The most memorable
stone in the cemetery is a monument inscribed *"Sacred to the
memory of 57 citizens of Truro who were lost in seven vessels, which
foundered at sea in the memorable gale of Oct 3, 1841."* Of the eight
Truro fishing vessels working Georges Bank about ninety miles off
Cape Cod, only one made it safely back to port. The storm claimed
the lives of ten percent of Truro's fishermen.

Losing men at sea was nothing new to the people of Truro. Some
six hundred Truro men were lost at sea over the one hundred-year
period from 1780 to 1880. Even at the turn of the twentieth century,
Truro counted more than one hundred widows among its population. But losing sailors were not the only losses Truro would suffer
over its history.

During the 1830s the town prospered from the sea, and the

Union Company Store at Pamet Harbor epitomized this prosperity. By 1860 a downturn fell upon the town and the Union Company, in which most Truro residents owned shares, went bankrupt. With little prospect for work, the 1840 population of 2,000 dropped to 1,000 residents by 1880. At the time of the Great Depression of the 1930s Truro's population bottomed out at 500 hardy souls.

Also built on the Hill of Churches was Union Hall, in 1830. That building became the town hall in 1840 and assumes the role to this day. Its architecture resembles that of a church and its spire seems to compete with the Congregational Church for its share of the heavens. As for the Methodists' meeting house, it was taken down in 1925 after ninety-nine years of service atop the Hill of Churches, remembered today only by a cemetery.

The Clay Pounds over at the Highlands on the east coast of Truro is a geological marvel that reminds one of the great Aquinnah cliffs of Martha's Vineyard. Deposited during the last ice age some ten to twenty thousand years ago, the six hundred-foot wide vein of blue clay erodes from the cliff wall in the vicinity of Highland Lighthouse. This vein runs clear across the Cape.

As for Highland Light, it was originally built atop the cliff in 1797 to provide mariners with a light to mark the dark coastline between Boston and Nantucket. The original tower was replaced with the current structure in 1857, and was moved back from the eroding cliff in 1996 to prevent its destruction. Today its majestic beam still sweeps some twenty miles out to sea, the first light to great transatlantic mariners approaching our shores.

And Truro's historic hills continue to rise above the valleys and marshes and moors, each peacefully and majestically moving us into the next century.

Monomoit – The Forsaken and Desolate

The settlement of Monomoit, today known as Chatham, happened in much the same way as at the other towns and villages across the Cape, by Indians some five thousand years ago.

Life for these Indians of Monomoit, Monomoyicks as they called themselves, was a simple yet structured existence - raising crops, hunting, fishing and possibly even whaling. They had a sachem (chief), and gods to which they prayed and land upon which they made their living. Their proud way of life could have continued for centuries, perhaps for millenniums.

But in October 1606, European explorers, including Jean de Poutrincourt, Samuel de Champlain and Daniel Hay, sailed into what is now Stage Harbor and anchored their vessel. With the dangerous shoals, these men of the French expedition were able to come ashore solely with the assistance of Indian guides. What followed was a preview of things to come.

The French, a bit unnerved by the large number of Indians, decided to give the Natives a display of their weaponry just to keep them in line. What resulted during the days to follow amounted to what "white" historians termed the first known Indian attack against Europeans on the northeast coast. It was the opening act to what would become the ultimate annihilation of the Indian nation during the latter half of the nineteenth century.

A battle erupted between the French and the Monomoyicks, ending in the deaths of a number of each and the later kidnapping and beheading of other Cape Indians by Champlain and his men. As could be expected, future relations between European explorers and the natives of Monomoit were much less friendly.

Famous European explorers like Henry Hudson, Samuel Argall, Edward Harlow, John Smith and Admiral Adrian Block sailed around the dangerous shoals of Monomoit. Some noted the "unfriendly" nature of the natives, others not bothering to stop at all because of the treacherous waters making this place undesirable to even the most adventurous.

Relations with the Monomoyicks were at an all time low in 1622 when Governor William Bradford of Plymouth arrived at Stage Harbor aboard the vessel *Swan* with Indian interpreter Squanto. With Squanto's assistance, Bradford was able to repair relations with the Monomoyicks and Squanto's sudden death at Monomoit brought even closer this new friendship.

The Monomoyick Indians suffered a number of setbacks during the seventeenth century, including a plague in 1616-17 that killed a large number of Indians across Cape Cod just prior to the Pilgrim's arrival. Smallpox outbreaks left the tribe nearly decimated when

Monomoit became a township in 1712.

Meanwhile, under the Bradford Patent of 1630, Cape Cod became part of the Plymouth Colony and the land became available to those who were termed "old-comers." These were settlers who came to the New World upon the *Mayflower* in 1620, the *Fortune* in 1621 or the *Anne* in 1623. To acquire land, the old-comers would simply buy out the Indians' interest, that is, if any Indians claimed ownership.

First step toward the settlement of Monomoit came in 1656 when William Nickerson of Yarmouth bought one hundred acres from the Monomoyick sachem Mattaquason in return for a boat, some tools, wampum and twelve shillings. But Nickerson was not an old-comer and his right to ownership was in dispute with the Colony Court. Though he settled in Monomoit in 1664, it was not until June 1672 when he actually received a deed symbolizing ownership.

Nickerson continued to acquire land from the Monomoyicks and by 1682 owned some four thousand acres, which was very nearly all of Monomoit. Unfortunately, people were not settling in this remote part of the Cape and for many years, through at least 1672, the members of the Nickerson family were the area's only white residents.

For taxation purposes Monomoit was placed under Yarmouth's domain in June 1668, and later under that of Eastham. When William Nickerson petitioned in 1675 that Monomoit become a township, his request was denied though the court did approve a request in March 1679 to allow Monomoit to separate itself from Eastham. Despite the fact that it was unable to locate a minister and thereby establish its own church, a prerequisite to becoming incorporated as a township, Monomoit was allowed by the court to handle its own affairs. Essentially, the residents could regulate their own system of taxation and Monomoit was granted the title of constablewich. Since it was still not considered a town it could not send representation to the Colony Court in Plymouth.

In 1690, Nickerson passed away at the age of eighty-five, leaving Monomoit without its founding father and religious leader. The very next year the constablewich became part of the Bay Colony and the area of Monomoit that he first settled some twenty-seven years earlier now had about two hundred residents. It possessed all the rights of a town, though it was still not incorporated.

As the years passed, the quest for incorporation coincided directly with the quest for a minister. It would take more than twenty years after William Nickerson's death to finally locate one. Reverend Samuel Treat of Eastham became Monomoit's spiritual leader in 1690, but only on a part-time basis. Reverend Nathaniel Stone of Harwich lent his services in 1696 and then, in 1697, Jonathon Vickery of Hull came to Monomoit. Vickery was not an ordained minister, but rather a lay preacher. By profession he was actually a fisherman. Regardless, the constablewich voted to pay him £20 per year if he would relocate to Monomoit and be its preacher. But tragedy struck in 1702 when Vickery and several town officials were drowned in a boating accident.

The search continued. For a £20 salary Mr. Gershom Hall of Harwich agreed to preach to the people of Monomoit, but negotiations to get him to relocate to the constablewich and become their personal minister failed. The list goes on with Reverend John Lattimer, Reverend Matthew Short, Reverend Jonathan Russell, Reverend Benjamin Allen and finally Reverend Hugh Adams in the spring of 1711.

Shortly after his arrival, Adams penned a petition to the General Court in June 1711. It asked that the men of Monomoit be excused from military draft to defend their families against French pirates and Indian attacks, that taxes be reduced, and that Monomoit be incorporated with an English name. In the petition, Adams wrote: "our congregation may be termed forsaken and desolate."

Adams' words must have reached compassionate ears for in January 1712 it was declared that "no men need be drafted from Monomoit for the military." Then, on June 11, 1712, the House of Representatives announced "that Monomoit be erected into a township and be called Chatham."

Normally, the story would end here with the incorporation of the town, but there is an interesting footnote to this story of Chatham concerning a legal battle involving two of the town's founding fathers - Reverend Hugh Adams and Selectman Ebenezer Hawes.

It all started when Adams accused Hawes of doing a poor job at running the town's only tavern. Hawes then said some things about Adams that caused the Reverend to sue the Chatham selectman for slander.

Hawes won the first legal battle and in June 1715 the town voted to oust Adams. Adams issued an appeal of the decision at Barnstable, but the court again found in favor of Hawes. A further appeal by Adams to the Superior Court of Judicature in Plymouth found in his favor. Despite the victory, Adams found that nearly everyone in town turned against him and did not wish him to be their minister.

In the spring of 1717, just five short years after he helped Chatham obtain its incorporation, the Reverend Hugh Adams left Chatham to spend the rest of his days in Durham, New Hampshire.

Anthony Thacher – Yarmouth's First Settler

In the village of Yarmouthport, just north of Route 6A, there is a footpath that winds its way in a northwesterly fashion through a beautiful Cape Cod wilderness of meadows and woodlands. Northward, beyond the conifers that grow here and there, spread the marshes that even further north surrender to the waters of Cape Cod Bay.

The trail leads to an opening in the woods where a large boulder can be found, seemingly lost and forgotten by the decades and centuries. Upon the boulder is a plaque and upon the plaque are these words:

Near this site lived and was buried Antony [sic] *Thacher*
He came to America in 1635 from Somersetshire, England
Shipwrecked on Thacher Island 1635
Settled in Yarmouth 1639

Many times a plaque on a boulder is the starting point for an historical journey, a fact-finding mission to discover a person or an event from the past and transport he or she or it to the present for us to study and marvel over. This Thacher must have been quite a local historical character to earn a plaque upon such a large boulder, never mind the fact that it is hidden away in the wilderness of Yarmouthport!

Anthony Thacher was, in fact, born in Somersetshire County, England around 1589. Like the Pilgrims, he was a Separatist and actually associated with a number of the Pilgrims at Leyden in Holland just ten years before the *Mayflower* sailed for Plymouth. Thacher would not sail with the Pilgrims, remaining behind to build a life, to marry and to father nine children. His Separatist views softened and he fell in with the established church, that being the Church of England. He meanwhile established himself, achieving a worthy social standing in his native England.

But Thacher's life was about to suffer the first of two setbacks. Five of his nine children would die of illness, followed by the death of his wife. Yet the very next year Thacher was remarried, to Elizabeth Jones, and was making plans to begin anew in Plymouth Colony. In April 1635, at the age of forty-six, Thacher, his new bride of six weeks, and his four surviving children sailed for the New World, arriving at Newbury in June.

Just two short months later further tragedy would strike the Thachers. While sailing from Ipswich to Marblehead with his cousin's family, their vessel was wrecked in a storm off Cape Ann. Of the twenty-three people on board, only Thacher and his wife survived. All four Thacher children were lost. Today, the island upon which Thacher and his new bride crawled to safety is still called Thatcher Island.

The court was so moved by the couple's loss that they were granted £26, 13 shillings and "fore-pence" to begin again. They would spend the next four years in Marblehead where their son John would be born in March 1639.

Meanwhile, during the previous year, Thacher surveyed land in the Mid-Cape area, land belonging to the Nobscusset Indians.

At the time that the Pilgrims arrived it is believed that the Cape population numbered between four and five thousand Indians comprising five tribes. Those five tribes included the Manamets, Shaumes and Suconessets of the Upper Cape area; the South Sea Indians of the Mid-Cape; and the Nausets of the Mid and Lower-

Cape regions.

All five Cape Cod tribes were members of the Wampanoag Indian Federation of which Massasoit was chief. Included in the Nauset tribe was the Nobscusset tribe of what is now Yarmouth and Dennis. Sachem of the Nobscusset at the time of the arrival of white settlers in 1639 was Mashantampaine.

On January 7, 1639, Thacher, along with fellow first settlers John Crow and Thomas Howes, were granted land "to take up their freedom at Yarmouth." At that time, Yarmouth, named for the English port, also contained what is today the town of Dennis.

One month after the birth of their son, the Thachers arrived at their new home in Yarmouth in April 1639. Thacher was immediately appointed to the land committee along with Crow and Howes and assigned the task of fairly dividing up the lands of Yarmouth amongst the newly arriving families. Thacher took 136 acres for himself, his land comprising most of the northwestern portion of the town.

Besides drawing up land deeds, Thacher also "executed conveyances, wills and other legal writings." He was town treasurer for twenty-eight years, deputy to the Colony Court for ten years and in 1655 was "appointed by the court to administer the ordinance of marriage at Yarmouth as occasion shall require."

He served on the council of war during Indian hostilities and in May 1657 he helped to draw up a land agreement known as the Yarmouth Acquittance with sachem Mashantampaine which essentially handed over the lands of the Nobscusset to Crow, Howe and Thacher.

Very soon, Mashantampaine and his people found themselves and their world evaporating before their eyes as more white settlers arrived to take the place of the natives who were dying off in record numbers due to disease. By the time Mashantampaine passed away, the Cape Indian population dwindled from four or five thousand to a mere one thousand natives. Just more than one hundred of those were from the Nobscusset tribe. A little more than one hundred years later the Nobscusset tribe was gone.

Besides serving as a teacher to the children of Yarmouth, in 1662 Thacher was "appointed inspector of anchors, lead, powder and

shot, as well as liquors" and in 1666 he was elected selectman. The
very next year Thacher departed these earthly bounds at nearly
eighty years of age. His son, John, would go on to father twenty-
one children, thus providing the town of Yarmouth with Thachers
enough for generations to come.

Reverend John Lothrop of Barnstable

Though he was not the first minister to arrive at Barnstable,
Reverend John Lothrop would be credited with contributing
greatly to the town's initial settlement. Actually, Reverend Joseph
Hull, who arrived from England in 1635, relocated himself and his
small congregation from Weymouth to Barnstable in mid-1639, just
a few months before Lothrop.

A religious separatist, Lothrop was jailed in England for two
years by the Bishop of London after a worship service he was
conducting in a private home was raided in 1632. Lothrop and his
congregation of thirty followers opted for banishment over further
persecution and sailed for the New World aboard the vessel *Griffin*
in 1634.

Arriving at Boston, they immediately settled in Scituate for the
next five years before moving on to Barnstable in October 1639. By
that time Lothrop's congregation grew to twenty-five families and
dwarfed Reverend Hull's much smaller following. Hull moved on
to Yarmouth, leaving Barnstable to Lothrop.

Before a meeting house was built, first church services were held
at a large boulder known as Sacrament Rock, also known as Pulpit
Rock. Though the boulder was later dynamited to make way for
Route 6A, pieces of the original rock were cemented together along
with a plaque to form a monument recognizing the spot where the
first services were held.

A twenty-one-foot by twenty-six-foot home was built for the
Reverend in 1644 to replace an earlier thatched roof house built
upon the year of settlement. The 1644 house was later expanded by
the Sturgis family in the eighteenth and nineteenth centuries and is
today a portion of the Sturgis Library, making it the oldest building in the country to be used as a library. On display at the library

Sacrament Rock along Route 6A in Barnstable, the site of Reverend Lothrop's first church services back in 1639. (J. Sheedy photo)

is Reverend Lothrop's 1605 bible that he brought over from England. While coming across on the *Griffin*, pages of the bible were burnt by dripping candle wax. Lothrop repaired the damaged pages and hand wrote the missing text from memory.

For fourteen years Reverend Lothrop preached to the people of Barnstable until his death in 1653 at the age of sixty-nine. In addition to Sacrament Rock and his bible on display at Sturgis Library, reminders of Reverend Lothrop can be found at two other spots. The Lothrop Hill Cemetery marks the site of the first meeting house while the West Parish Meeting House on Route 149, built in 1717, remains a direct descendant of the church of the original settlers.

William Apes & Mashpee's War for Independence

Mashpee is unique among all towns on Cape Cod because of its close association with the Wampanoag Federation of Native

Americans. Known by many as Cape Cod's "Indian town,"
Mashpee boasts a history of administrative home rule by indigenous people. But the route to self-government by the Indians of
Mashpee was a lengthy and difficult one and it was accomplished
in the face of long-established white paternalism and outright
racism.

   From the earliest days of white settlement on Cape Cod, native
people were continuously squeezed and relocated from their
traditional lands to the point where, by the beginning of the
eighteenth century, there were few survivors of what was a once
numerous and vigorous people. Though they kept a loose tribal
structure, the Wampanoag people were submerged by an English
colonial structure that took little notice of their culture or their
needs.

   In the late 1600s "Marshpee," as it was then called, became a
settlement area for the Indian survivors of King Philip's War. In
1763 the area was incorporated as a plantation. White colonial
administrators were appointed to control the affairs of the district
because it was felt that the native people were incapable of running their own affairs. The Indians had no say as to who would be
their overseers. It can be said that their status was not unlike that
of the vassalage of medieval European serfs. No schools were set
up to educate the Wampanoags and their children were commonly
"bound out" as indentured laborers to the farms of local whites.

   Several attempts were made to create some form of home rule
prior to the Revolutionary War but with the exception of a few
gratuitous and relatively meaningless gestures from the Crown,
there was no real effort to create any sort of self-government for
native people on Cape Cod. When the Revolution ended, the new
government of Massachusetts moved quickly to reaffirm white
control in the district.

   After years of fruitless petitioning, the arrival in May 1833 of a
self-educated Methodist Pequot preacher named William Apes
signaled the beginning of renewed hope for some sort of home
rule. Apes was an itinerant missionary who moved about New
England after running away from his indenture in Connecticut. He
was originally from Colrain, Massachusetts, and apparently

decided to come to Mashpee out of curiosity about the Native American community there.

Apes became immediately involved in the issue of home rule as both an organizer and a publicist. The effect of his arrival and settlement in Mashpee emboldened the Indian people in Mashpee. Almost a half-century after white America gained its independence, the Wampanoags made another concerted effort to gain theirs. With Apes as their inspirational leader, a twelve man Indian council was elected that drafted what amounted to a nullification document challenging the established guardianship laws of the Mashpee district.

It was common practice for white residents of neighboring towns to go at will into the Indian district and take wood and shellfish without regard to Indian property rights. Whites helped themselves to Mashpee's shellfish beds and pasturage. Because the authority to lease out grazing and haying lands was in the hands of the non-Indian overseers, complaints by native people to stop the practice went unheeded.

On May 21, 1833, led by Apes and Baptist minister "Blind Joe" Amos, the Wampanoags drew up a formal protest that paralleled the U.S. Constitution. Its most aggressive clause called for self-rule, because, as it stated, "all men are born free and equal, as says the Constitution of our country." In addition, the resolution declared that native people "would not permit any white man to come upon our Plantation, to cut, or to carry off, wood, or hay, or any other article, without our permission, after the 1st of July next."

Adding a supporting clause for good measure, the manifesto threatened to deal with violators by "binding them and throwing them out!" Two hundred eighty-seven Mashpee residents out of a permanent population of just more than three hundred signed the resolution, praying for the basic privilege to manage their own property.

For a Cape Cod that had not seen any local Indian difficulties for almost two centuries, the publication of this bold document was seen as an insurrection. References to the so-called "Woodlot War" cropped up in the local press and Massachusetts Governor Levi Lincoln prepared to call out the state militia.

On July 1, 1833 a group of whites led by William Samson of
Barnstable went into the Wampanoag district to take wood and
there was a confrontation. The Wampanoags moved to enforce
their control over their property. Reverend Apes was arrested with
several other native men, taken to Cotuit and charged with "riot,
assault, and trespass." The last charge was levied against Apes
because he never received the permission of the white overseers to
become a legal resident of the district. After a guilty verdict, he
was sentenced to thirty days in jail and a fine of one hundred
dollars. Lemuel Ewer, a white farmer from South Sandwich posted
the $200 bail for Apes who was allowed to return to Mashpee to
await a date for imprisonment.

In an effort to prevent an escalation of the problems in Mashpee,
Governor Lincoln sent a delegation to mediate the dispute. Almost
all of the whites in Barnstable County stood with the overseers.
William Apes was portrayed by most of the press as an outside
agitator and manipulator. No Cape legislator was willing to
introduce the Indian resolution before the General Court. Osterville lawyer Benjamin Hallett eventually argued the nullification
case in the state legislature for the Wampanoags and, aided by a
speech by Apes, convinced the body that the guardianship of the
district was outdated and indeed, patently unfair to the native
people who lived in Mashpee.

In March of 1834, the plantation was given the status of a self-
governing district and the Wampanoags were allowed for the first
time to elect their own selectmen.

It would be thirty-six more years before Mashpee was granted a
charter in 1870 to become an incorporated town on Cape Cod. In
the interim, William Apes seemed to gradually lose his position of
leadership in the Indian community. His name shows up in county
records for failure to pay taxes, perhaps indicating difficult economic circumstances. He lived for some years in South Mashpee
near Dean's Pond but he fades from the town and county records
after 1838. What happened to him is still a mystery. The man who,
perhaps more than any other, could be said to be the prime catalyst
for Mashpee's independence returned into the obscurity from
whence he came.

Chapter
2

Walking, Warning Out & Watering Troughs

Our ancestors were truly amazing people. They took what the earth offered and fashioned a life from her simple gifts.

As early settlers, they battled for their very existence every day. From the land and the sea they harvested their sustenance. From the forests they took trees to build houses, churches, and sailing vessels. And once the wilds were tamed they battled with their neighbors instead over property boundaries and religion.

The pages of history point to the curious customs of "disorderly walking" and "warning out" that were practiced in colonial times in an attempt to keep religious order and discourage the settlement of "undesirables." Meanwhile, some families decided to pack up and leave the Cape altogether, moving away in large groups to settle towns in distant states as the country pushed outward toward new horizons.

The Colonial Custom of "Warning Out"

New Englanders have always been accused of being a bit reserved when it comes to neighbors. Unlike our more sociable southern cousins, New England families can often live together on the same street for years and still never have any close contact … maybe not even to the point of a "hello." There is almost a feeling that, in these parts, a person has to do something special or extraordinary to be finally "accepted."

This anti-social New England character has some basis in history. A look at the colonial records of Cape Cod when it was part of the Plymouth Colony shows the curious practice of "warning out" of potential new settlers who were, for various reasons, considered potentially undesirable neighbors. The custom was transferred from England along with a number of long-standing land codes that came with colonization.

In the old country, it was customary that a village would accept the responsibility for the conduct and support of each other, sort of an "each for all and all for each" idea. The old English term was "frank-pledge" which roughly translated meant that if towns were corporations established by free consent, then it was the right of these free inhabitants to deny residency to those that were not considered desirable.

Even with all of the open space that was available in the early Plymouth Colony, the incorporated towns reserved the right to approve or disapprove of potential residents. Perhaps more than anything else, the idea of "warning out" was centered on the custom that, once granted the right of inhabitancy, a person was also granted the right to be supported by the town if the person later became unable to support himself.

Without legal inhabitancy an individual had no status in a town. Violators were warned that they had "no power to act in any town meeting till better evidence appear of their legal admittance; nor to claim title or interest to any town privileges as town's men" until their settlement was officially approved.

In 1661, Richard Child was ordered by the court of Plymouth Colony to "desist from building a cottage at Yarmouth." In the same year, Sandwich passed a town meeting article stating that "two persons have power to take notice of such as would intrude themselves into the town without the town's consent and prevent them residing there."

In 1666, the Plymouth Colony, which by then included the Cape Cod towns of Sandwich, Barnstable, Yarmouth, and Eastham, passed a law that required the approval of the governor and two assistants before the right of inhabitancy could be granted. Laws were also passed prohibiting owners of land or houses from selling to a stranger without the consent of the individual town inhabitants. Some towns even went so far as to fine or censure inhabitants who received strangers into their homes.

The actual enforcement of these inhabitation laws varied among the towns. Some towns were very strict and warned all newcomers as a matter of course, recording the warning in the Court of Sessions as a protection against liability. But exceptions were often made and some people were admitted with conditions. There may, for example, have been a need for a certain trade in a particular town. As long as the stranger held "inoffensive carriage," his presence was tolerated. Charging a surety bond was also a common practice so that a town would not have to pay support in the future.

By the beginning of the eighteenth century, as the population of New England began to grow rapidly, the desire of persons to move to new lands in the colonies made it more difficult to enforce the inhabitancy laws. In November of 1692, shortly after the Plymouth Colony was combined with Massachusetts, a law was passed that made a simple public posting of a "warning" to be legally sufficient notice that a town would not have to assume liability for the support of poor individuals. Constables were directed by selectmen to post these warnings in public places.

A law eight years later noted that, "If any person not an inhabitant, orderly warned to depart, and sent by warrant of a Justice of the Peace to the town where he properly belonged or to the place of his last abode, should come back to the town from which he had been warned and sent, he should be proceeded against as a vagabond."

In the period following the American Revolution, the inhabitancy laws gradually faded away. In 1793 all such laws directly related to the practice of "warning out" were repealed in Massachusetts. But there are examples that showed that the practice didn't die easily. In 1810, Edward O'Brien was denied the position of postmaster in the town of Brewster and encouraged to leave town because of "he being a foreigner, a catholik {sic} and, in the opinion of the town, an alien." As late as the 1830s town meeting approval of legal settlement was still required by some Cape Cod towns.

Perhaps today such a practice seems a bit narrow and cliquish. It is difficult to deny that "warning out" didn't contain elements of both. But the next time one of your neighbors revs up his chain saw on an early Sunday morning, or the dog in the adjacent yard continues to bark for nights on end, remember that there once was a very simple remedy for those who do not always practice "inoffensive carriage."

The Strange Crime of "Disorderly Walking"

During the early days of settlement, the inhabitants of Cape Cod, like the rest of Colonial New England, were expected to be strong followers of the established Congregational Church. The civil government, operating much like a theocracy, strictly enforced orthodoxy.

A minister served each town, drawing his support, fiscal as well as spiritual, from the local community of believers. Some of these ministers were legendary. The town of Dennis, for example, so esteemed their beloved minister, Josiah Dennis, that they named the town after him.

In Eastham, the Reverend Samuel Treat served the town during the late seventeenth and early eighteenth centuries, a total of forty-three years, all the while preaching Christian values and guiding the souls of Native Indians and citizens along the path of righteousness on the Outer Cape. Clearly, he was a difficult act to follow.

When he died in 1717, the resulting vacancy of the pulpit created a theological situation that pitted citizens against each other, splitting the Eastham religious community and even permanently dividing families.

In 1719, as part of an effort to block the ordination of the Reverend Samuel Osborn of Sandwich as the new minister in Eastham, Mrs. Hannah Doane, along with others, signed a protest letter against the installation. The petition did not sit well with the all-male church deacons, who charged Mrs. Doane with the crime of "disorderly walking."

This was an ordinance against separating from the established church without first obtaining permission from town authorities. Mrs. Doane was apparently singled out as a high-profile leader in the movement to stop the Reverend Osborn's accession to the pulpit.

Sensing she would get no satisfaction from the deacons, many of whom expressed private opinions that she was a habitual malcontent, Mrs. Doane duly requested a proper dismissal from the church. The deacons agreed to grant her request, but only if she signed a paper stating that she was being dismissed for immoral conduct! She refused to sign this document and was subsequently charged additionally with being "a common disturber of the peace."

The deacons followed this with a statement claiming that Mrs. Doane showed "contempt for the church's lenity," and a "usurpation of that power and liberty which Christ has denied your sex to speak in church."

With this, Mrs. Doane and her supporters called for a countywide ecclesiastical council to be held at Yarmouth in the fall of 1720. This assembly, which consisted of most of the ordained ministers of Cape Cod, evaluated the evidence presented by both sides of the controversy and determined that the Eastham deacons were guilty of "Maladministration" and that they essentially owed the woman an apology.

Mrs. Doane, perhaps gloating in her victory, wrote to the deacons stating that if they publicly confessed their errors, she would gladly acknowledge her faults publicly if, she concluded, she had any!

In anger, the Eastham church summarily excommunicated Mrs. Doane. This action brought a judgment from the ecclesiastical council to excommunicate the entire Eastham church!

Eventually, the matter was worked out as cooler heads pre-

vailed. Mrs. Doane was granted her dismissal from the Eastham
church and Reverend Osborn was able to take the pulpit in the
south parish of Eastham where he preached for some years.

But perhaps the more important outcome of the controversy was
that the 1720 council ruling was used as a later precedent in the
area of personal conscience matters and in the slowly expanding
role of women in the church.

Cape Cod Smallpox Cemeteries

Two hundred years ago such symptoms as high fever and
vomiting, along with a headache, muscle pains and a rash of red
blisters on the head and limbs would point to the dreaded pox.

Smallpox has been the scourge of humanity since prehistoric
times. Throughout the centuries there were large outbreaks. The
early settlers of this area and even the Native Indians were not
immune to its ravages. In fact, smallpox was one of the contributing factors leading to the annihilation of the Cape and Islands
Indians who, by the mid-nineteenth century, were all but gone
save for tribes in Mashpee and at Aquinnah on Martha's Vineyard.

The viral disease, which resembled cowpox, was highly infectious
and could be contracted by either direct contact with a carrier or by
touching the bedclothes or clothing of someone infected. Between
thirty and forty percent of those who contracted smallpox would die.

In the days before medicines there was no treatment for the
disease, only bed rest, fluids and sedatives to make the victim as
comfortable as possible. If the victim survived, their skin would
most likely be permanently marked by the pox.

The only preventive method was the isolation of the sick from
the other members of the village, the quick burial of the deceased,
and the burning or burial of the victim's clothing and bedclothes.
So feared was this pox that those who died from the disease were
buried by family members on their property rather than in the
village cemetery, or else in the case of large epidemics, in a designated plot for smallpox victims. These burial sites, though very
difficult to find, dot the Cape and send their messages across the
centuries of the hardships our ancestors bore.

This Yarmouthport smallpox cemetery dating to 1801 is located at the 13th hole of the Kings Way Golf Course. (J. Sheedy photo)

A tour of these smallpox cemeteries upon a spring day can be a somber journey. These lonely smallpox markers in nearly forgotten spots, rather than in the populated village burial grounds, can chime a bell of sadness in one's heart.

The first visit is to the grave of a Chatham doctor who fought the dreaded disease that ravaged his fellow townsfolk ... and in the end he too succumbed to its death grip. Along the side of Training Field Road rests his stone, resting perhaps no more than two feet from the paved street where today automobiles speed past, their passengers unaware of its historical significance. The stone reads: *"Here lies buried Dr. Samuel Lord who died of smallpox after devoted service to the citizens of Chatham in the epidemic of 1765-66."*

Not far from Dr. Lord's grave rest a number of his patients in a smallpox cemetery off Old Comers Road. It is a shaded lot perhaps one hundred feet in from the road where a half dozen stones rest, encircled by concrete posts supporting metal rails. The wooded lot, so peaceful with a slight breeze tickling the leaves above and with the calling of birds, is today a sharp contrast to the horror and sadness of those months from December 1765 to March 1766 when ten percent of the town's population contracted the disease. Twenty-four of those infected survived while thirty-seven others died.

Considered one of the Cape's worst outbreaks, it is believed the seeds of pestilence arrived in Chatham in either a shipment of clothing from the West Indies or a bale of cotton from a southern state. Typically, smallpox was detected early and contained to a handful of infected persons or a family, but in the Chatham case it somehow was allowed to spread until it reached epidemic proportions. Before it ended the disease claimed not only the local doctor but also the deacon and a doctor from neighboring Harwich as he tried to combat the devilish disease.

During one horrible week, between January 11 and 17, seventeen deaths occurred. Boston physicians and medical support staffs arrived on the scene. With the death of Mrs. Mehitabel Rider on March 20th the horror finally ended.

At this particular cemetery on Old Comers Road, there is a stone belonging to *"Mrs. Mercy Doane, the wife of Mr. Joseph Doane Junior, She Dec'd with the smallpox Jan'ry ye 6th 1766 in ye 25th year of her age."*

Of the other stones, one belongs to the Deacon Stephen Smith who died on January 13 at the age of sixty. Another belongs to his wife who fell victim to the disease just three days later: *"Here lies buried Mrs. Bathsheba Smith, widow to Mr. Stephen Smith, who Dec'd in ye 57th year of her age with the smallpox, She Dec'd Jan'ry ye 16th 1766."* They also lost two daughters to the disease.

Also resting here are the mortal remains of Stephen Rider who, along with his wife and nine of their ten children, *"died with the smallpox."*

The town of Orleans has a smallpox grave on Tar Kiln Road, while the town of Dennis has two locations. One grave is that of a child located in the woods where Setucket and Airline roads meet. Another gravesite is located on Summer Street in the village of Dennisport. The stone, which was small and white, is gone now. It held the name *"J. Wixon."* Now the gravesite is merely a section of somebody's front lawn. Who is to know how many of our properties contain the ashes of pioneers, perhaps even smallpox victims!

Yarmouthport contains a couple of smallpox grave locations. A gravesite on Follins Pond just east of North Dennis Road contains

A number of those who died in the epidemic of 1765-66 are buried at this smallpox cemetery located along Old Comers Road in Chatham. (J. Sheedy photo)

three stones and the dust of four smallpox victims. One stone is for John Eldredge who died of the disease on January 6, 1797 at the age of fifty-four. Isaac Matthews, sixty-one years old, died on December 15 of the previous year. The third stone, marked "E.T." and "S.T.," is thought to belong to Elizabeth Taylor and Sarah Taylor, who died on January 13, 1797.

Those golfing at the Kings Way course in Yarmouthport can view a smallpox cemetery on the 13th hole. Just a short pitching wedge shot from the green rest two stones encircled by a rusted chain draping from granite posts driven into the four corners of the small plot. Buried here are John Hall, who died on December 14, 1801 at the age of sixty-four, and a person by the name of Taylor (the stone is largely illegible).

Smallpox was such a problem at the turn of the nineteenth century, at the time of the outbreak that took John Hall's life, that the town of Yarmouth voted to build a smallpox inoculation house on Great Island off in Nantucket Sound, far from the population of the town.

Provincetown, with its seafaring traffic transporting people from all over the world to her docks, was a breeding ground for all types of diseases. Many people would come off a ship ill to die a short time later, their body buried in the sands at the end of the

Cape. So it is no surprise that Provincetown has a number of smallpox graves, many being unmarked, identity unknown.

Finally, English physician Edward Jenner (1749-1823) determined that a cowpox inoculation would prevent smallpox. In 1775 he noticed that dairymaids who were infected with cowpox did not contract smallpox. He then began to perform experiments; one involved inoculating his own son with cowpox and then introducing him to the smallpox virus! Thankfully, his son did not become infected. In 1798 Jenner published *Inquiry into the Cause and Effects of the Variolae Vaccinae*, thus announcing to the world that the smallpox vaccine had been discovered.

Today, smallpox has been wiped from the globe. All that remain of its ravages are the lonely stones planted here and there in quiet and forgotten spots, and the sad stories told by their chiseled words.

Village Pumps & Watering Troughs

Wander through the main streets of any Cape town and you are bound to find an old village pump or stone watering trough by the side of the road pointing to an earlier age. In Dennis, there is a pump and trough located on the Dennis village green at the corner of Route 6A and Old Bass River Road. The date on the granite trough is 1891 and the pump itself still draws water.

Another trough, a few hundred feet away, rests next to the Dennis Union Church. It is also dated 1891 and now sits next to a display housing the old bell from the Dennis Grade School that once stood in this location from 1859 to 1931. Further south, a green pump and granite watering trough located on the grounds of the Jericho House in South Dennis is dated 1888. It once stood along the main route in West Dennis. A second pump is also located on the grounds at Jericho.

Along Route 6A in Brewster, just one hundred feet east of the Brewster Store, is a pump accented with an arch of stone towering over it. The trough proudly reads *"Brewster 1902."*

Perhaps the best known of all Cape pumps is the Simpkins Memorial Pump at the corner of Route 6A and Summer Street in Yarmouthport near the Olde Yarmouth Inn. The pump and granite

The Brewster Village Pump. (J. Sheedy photo)

trough date back to 1886. Around the pump is a wrought iron memorial erected *"In memory of Nathaniel Stone Simpkins, 1861-1919, Friend of Mankind, Kind to Man's Friends"* as the inscription on the back reads. The memorial was *"Given to the town of Yarmouth by his wife Mabel Jenks Simpkins, 1928."* Nathaniel Simpkins was a great animal lover as evidenced by the inscription on the back of the memorial and the images of birds, horses and dogs that comprise the wrought iron structure.

The town of Barnstable has a number of memorials to honor our ancestors' watering needs. In the old village is a water trough in front of the Olde Colonial Courthouse at the corner of Route 6A and Rendezvous Lane. In Marstons Mills, out in front of the Cash Market, is a black Red Jacket brand pump and a trough below which now serves as a planter. Another trough supporting flowers these days instead of water is at the war memorial green in the village of Centerville, at the intersection of Main Street, Park Avenue and Old Stage Road.

Located across the street from the First Congregational Church in Harwich, where Route 124 meets Route 39, is a trough dated 1904. Along Main Street in Chatham center, right in front of the

First Methodist Church on the corner of Cross Street, is an 1895
Red Jacket pump *"erected by the Village Improvement Club - 1914."*
Orleans also has a pump made in 1895 by the Red Jacket Manufacturing Company of Davenport, Iowa. Like the Chatham pump, it is
of the two-inch tubular variety. The Orleans pump, painted red
and white, is located along Route 28 across from Namequoit Road.

Before the Cape's oldest windmill, in Eastham, can be found a
trough with the year 1905 carved onto its granite base and the
words *"Blessed are the merciful."* Arriving in Wellfleet Center at the
intersection of Bank and Commercial streets one can view the
beautiful town pump on display there. The front and back of the
white stone trough read *"Town Center"* in black lettering with an
equally black arrow pointing up Bank Street, while the west side
of the trough reads *"Pier"* with an arrow pointing down toward
Commercial Street.

Besides providing water, these village pumps provided a central
gathering place where neighbors might meet and exchange the
news of the day while filling their buckets and watering their
animals. Today, these same village pumps and troughs provide us
with a tangible link to the past.

The "Come Outers" of Cape Cod

Contrary to what you may immediately assume, this is not a
story about Cape Codders who went public about their sexual
orientation. The "Come Outers" were actually a radical Christian
religious sect of the early nineteenth century that drew inspiration
from the "Great Awakening" movement that brought a renewed
religious fervor to much of New England.

Sometimes referred to as "New Lights," their brand of religious
expression espoused much enthusiasm and was seen by the more
conservative main line Christian community as often bordering on
the bizarre. Come Outers took their name from the Bible; 2nd
Corinthians 7-16, "What agreement hath the temple of God with
idols? Wherefore come out from among them and be ye separate."

The movement was characterized by a rejection of anything that
smacked of worldliness. Religious services usually held in private

homes and occasionally outdoors were marked by highly emotional behavior expressed by wild singing and shouting. Believing that the things of this world constituted a source of idolatry, no ornamentation of any kind within the home was approved. Fringes were cut off drapes, mirrors were turned to the wall, even figured wallpaper was torn up. The story is told of a handsome four-poster bedstead that had its carved posts sheared off cleanly with a saw by the owner!

Adherents to the Come Outer philosophy were known to disrupt some orthodox church services. For this they were often arrested and fined. Later, many members became associated with the abolition movement and for a time made anti-slavery an important part of their cause. On Cape Cod they were always a small group. By the end of the Civil War, with age probably bringing moderation to their views, they either became absorbed by other various "isms," joined Pentecostal-type churches, or disappeared entirely.

The Search for Greener Pastures

Perhaps as interesting as the study of those who first settled on the Cape is the study of those who left this beautiful peninsula to settle in other regions of the United States, and even in Canada.

A number of Cape towns, particularly Yarmouth and Chatham, experienced an exodus during the eighteenth century. Handfuls of families departed for greener pastures elsewhere. In some cases they returned to the Cape, but in most cases they did not.

Such an emigration from the Cape resulted in the settlement of Gorham, Maine in 1736 by the descendants of Captain John Gorham of Yarmouth and a large number of others from Yarmouth as well as from Barnstable, Eastham, Truro, Falmouth and Sandwich. The land was granted by the legislature of Massachusetts in 1727 to those who served in the Narragansett expedition during the King Philip's War some fifty years earlier, or if no longer living, then to their legal heirs. In fact, Captain John Gorham himself died at Swansea, Massachusetts in 1676 shortly after his battle with Narragansett Indians and it was his grandson Shubael Gorham who obtained the land grants to what would become Gorham, Maine.

Townships in the province of Maine were set aside for this

purpose, each township six square miles in area to contain one
hundred and twenty people each. Some eight hundred and forty
people claimed entitlement, so seven townships were arranged,
each called Narragansett followed by a number from one to seven.
The Gorham party received Narragansett No. 7, just west of
Portland. Families who helped to settle the township included all
the names familiar to us as Yarmouth families: Thacher, Hallett,
Matthew, Hall, Taylor, Gage, Wing, Gray, Baker, Crowell and
Baxter. Also, some very familiar Barnstable names were included:
Phinney, Cobb, Bacon and Sturgis. All these Cape names repre-
sented the founding fathers of the town of Gorham, Maine.

A second exodus from Yarmouth took place during the years of
the Revolutionary War. Twenty families, among them Howes,
Eldredges, Halls and Sears, left their Cape Cod home for the town of
Ashfield out in western Massachusetts. Smaller migrations occurred
into the nineteenth century with a small group following Reverend
Timothy Alden Jr. to Meadville, Pennsylvania in 1817, and handfuls
of people settling in New York, Illinois and further west.

There is even a town out in Nebraska called Hyannis. The village
of Hyannis on Cape Cod received its name as either a misspelling,
mispronunciation or misinterpretation of the name of the Mid-Cape
Indian sachem Iyanough. So how is it that a town in Nebraska
should receive the same strange name, unless someone familiar with
Hyannis on Cape Cod had something to do with it? A casual glance
at the Nebraska map also reveals towns called Brewster, Orleans,
Plymouth and Wellfleet, as well as counties called Chase, Gage and
Hall. Perhaps just coincidences, but maybe not. After all, a Cape
Nickerson did, in fact, settle Nickerson, Nebraska.

The town of Chatham saw many migrations, one taking place just
a year before the town's incorporation in 1712, leaving only thirty or
so families remaining. This 1711 exodus saw thirteen families leave
the area for various reasons. For a long period the settlement of
Monomoit (now Chatham) lacked an established church, and
without a church the settlement could not become incorporated as a
township. Also, residents of the area were upset about the taxes they
were forced to pay as well as the constant threat of French pirates
invading the area. A number of the families who left Monomoit at

this period settled at Duck Creek (now called Smyrna), Delaware. This emigration included Nickersons and Eldredges as well as families from other Cape towns including Truro.

A second emigration from Chatham, in 1747, saw many Nickersons, Covells, Eldredges, Taylors, Howes and Ryders join Yarmouth and Harwich families who earlier settled in 1740 along the New York/Connecticut border at a region called the Oblong, part of Putnam county.

The years 1760 to 1763 saw a third emigration from the town of Chatham. This exodus involved some fifty Chatham families, joining many other people from all over Cape Cod and Nantucket, moving to Liverpool and Barrington, Nova Scotia to replace the French who were forced by the British to leave the area in 1755 during the French and Indian War. About three hundred Chatham people were involved in this move, roughly a third of the town's population. Two years later a smallpox epidemic swept through Chatham, infecting ten percent of its remaining population. Who knows how many of those who left for Nova Scotia would have died with the pox had they stayed in Chatham!

Chatham's fourth emigration started around 1790 with a large number of families moving to the Penobscot River area of Maine. The settlement names consisted of Orphans Island, Orrington, Mount Vernon, Buckstown and Orland. In 1795 another large move saw former Chatham residents relocating to the Kennebec River region of Maine, most of them settling in Readville, about fifty miles north of Portland.

Every town has its "old comers," its first settlers. For whatever reason, people felt the urge to uproot from more familiar surroundings and settle a new area, knowing their new lives would most likely be filled with hardship and uncertainty. Perhaps it is human nature to attempt to improve one's situation, if not for one's own benefit then for that of the generations to follow.

Tourist Season of a Century Ago

The arrival of summer on Cape Cod and the Islands has traditionally been a time for outdoor activities centered around our greatest resource and attraction - the seashore.

And for year-round residents, "the season," as it is known, would not be complete without the large number of tourists that come with it. This tide of summer visitors has been with us for more than a hundred years. In the late-nineteenth century, following the completion of the railroad to Provincetown, and regular steamship connections to this area, the Cape and Islands became a destination for those who had the money and the leisure time to experience a seaside vacation.

While the attraction was then, as it is today, the beaches and ocean, in many ways the tourist season of a century ago reflected different themes and different values. Even the summer visitors themselves were different. The concept of taking a vacation was still alien to most Americans. The weekend as we now know it did not exist. With the vast majority of people still living in rural areas and without the disposable income necessary to even consider taking some time off, the tourist class that visited the Cape and Islands was decidedly well-heeled.

The grand hotels that proliferated here after 1880 were built to satisfy the summer requirements of this upper class of tourists who came, not for just a few days or a week, but for the entire season.

The Cape Cod Division of the New York, New Haven, and Hartford Railroad began its summer schedule in the third week of June, with six daily trains to Cape Cod. Vacationers arrived at the train depots with their large steamer trunks and were met by local drivers who brought them to the beachfront resorts.

Local people baked the pies, made the beds, and supplied the fresh foods for these vacationers and watched with no little awe as the visitors played tennis and golf, attended concerts and clambakes, and learned to sail.

Some tourists rented cottages or occupied houses that had names like "Sunnydale," "Grandview," or "Nestle-down" and settled in to the end of August. Newspapers reported who had arrived for the season. *"The Misses Bayles of Orange, New Jersey are at the 'Bayles Cottage' formerly the 'Copeland Place,' we hope for the season."*

"Mr. Joseph Patterson of New York has taken Sunnybank Cottage."

THE NOBSCUSSETT, DENNIS, MASS

Depicted on this old postcard is the grand hotel Nobscussett on the bay in Dennis, named for the Indians of the area. (J. Coogan Collection)

Even the guests at the hotels found their names listed in the paper and were no doubt socially gratified to know that they had been noticed.

The summer of 1897 was by accounts warm and relatively dry. There was hardly any rain for most of July until the end of the month when heavy rains and a strong wind caused some shorefront damage. The daily temperatures ranged from a low of 60 degrees to a high of 90 with the average in the mid-70s. August was a repeat of July with its own good rain and lightning storm on the 16th.

Newspapers advertised beach toys for the children ... pails, sand mills, shovels, and fishing tackle. Ice cream parlors opened at two in the afternoon and stayed open until late in the evenings. It seemed that bicycling was the rage and baseball games and horse racing drew large crowds. Yacht races were held in both Cape Cod Bay and Nantucket Sound and considerable money changed hands at the weekly sailboat races on Pleasant Lake in Harwich and Wequaquet Lake in Barnstable.

Both the railroad and the steamship companies added special

excursions to different area attractions, boosting the number of visitors.

On one Saturday afternoon in July the 1:40 p.m. train into Hyannis unloaded 792 passengers, creating a large jam of drivers and teams on Main Street. *The Barnstable Patriot* noted in the July 19, 1897 edition that *"All Cape Trains have been full to overflowing this week. And the baggage!"*

One anonymous short rhyme summed up the arrival of the season.

"The summer boarders are on the way,
With plenty of money and 10 weeks to stay;
They'll find the Cape a delightful spot,
Where it's neither too cool nor yet too hot."

Some tourists were visiting the Cape and Islands for religious reasons. The Cape Cod Association of Spiritualists was hosting its annual camp meeting in Ocean Grove in Harwichport during the last two weeks of July. The Yarmouth Camp Meeting Gospel Wagon began its trek from Truro to Yarmouth where it would arrive by the first of August. The Craigville Camp Meeting in Centerville was heavily subscribed and the Baptist Association was meeting at Cottage City on Martha's Vineyard.

For those whose destination was one of the grand hotels like the Nobscusset in Dennis, the Chequesset Inn in Wellfleet, or the Hotel Chatham on Pleasant Bay in Chatham, the accommodations were as refined as the guests themselves.

The Hotel Chatham, for example, advertised that it offered *"every modern convenience - open fireplaces and spacious halls, billiard rooms, bowling alleys, tennis courts, etc."*

At the Nobscusset on Cape Cod Bay, where there were accommodations for one hundred and fifty guests, vacationers could take advantage of a golf course and a fine stretch of beach with a long wooden pier where *"the pleasures of salt water bathing could be enjoyed by the guests."* The owners claimed that the local drinking water exceeded the quality and taste of the famous Poland Springs of Maine, and they advertised a doctor who certified that no one ever got hay fever in Dennis.

For those who desired an alcohol-free vacation, the Chequesset

Inn was a "dry" hotel. Set on the pilings of an old fishing pier, the Chequesset offered *"the pleasant and health giving advantages of a sea voyage, with none of the drawbacks."* Among the attractions, the Chequesset advertised *"fresh and saltwater baths, running water, electric lights, electric bells, telephones, and pure spring water."* Incidentally, the owner shut off the primitive electric light system every night promptly at 10:30 p.m. because it was his belief that by this late in the evening, all respectable people should be in bed!

As the first of September approached, the final event of the summer featured the County Agricultural Fair. Visitors and local residents crowded the fairgrounds in Barnstable village to see the horse races, the ball games, and the exhibits. In 1897 the major attraction was a balloon ascension, one of the first ever attempted on Cape Cod.

And then, almost as quickly as it began, the season was over. The cottages were closed up, as were the great hotels, and Cape Cod reverted to its comfortable isolation. The train schedule was reduced and large estates were returned to the trust of local caretakers. There was no "shoulder season" or even an Indian summer. The fall brought the harvest time and the prime hunting season. For local people it was an occasion to perhaps laugh about the peculiarities of the recently departed visitors and to begin to put things away in readiness for the long "off season" that would follow.

Chapter 3

Enterprising Cape Codders

Just as today, in order to survive Cape Codders needed to find suitable employment. The Cape economy down through the centuries offered them many opportunities.

Earliest settlers were farmers, but the Cape soil left much to be desired. A greater harvest was calling to them - the harvest of the ocean. So the Cape farmers became fishermen.

Mackerel and cod were the staples of the Cape fishing industry. Dennisport, Harwich and Truro prospered with the full nets of their fishing fleets. Leading the way, though, was Provincetown and its Portuguese fishermen. In the mid-nineteenth century there were more than one hundred fishing boats operating out of Provincetown Harbor alone. Fish flakes would line the wharves with the catch drying under the sun, filling the air with the most pungent aromas of their success.

Yet, despite the Cape's inferior soil, Falmouth somehow managed to become the largest producer of strawberries east of the Mississippi. Through it all, Cape entrepreneurs persevered.

Oysters, Iron Ore and Ox Carts

Because of its rich oyster beds, the Cape township known as Billingsgate was renamed Wellfleet after Wallfleet, England - another coast town known for its population of oysters. In 1602, explorer Samuel Champlain first named the Lower Cape harbor Port aux Huitres, which translates as Port of Oysters. Though the Wellfleet oyster beds died off during an epidemic in the 1770s, they were re-seeded after the Revolutionary War to become even richer than ever, making Wellfleet Massachusetts' largest producer.

• • •

Indians were, of course, the first to discover the shelled delicacies that populated the flats at low tide. The early settlers followed their lead. Shellfish of the Cape served a number of purposes, as food, bait and even fertilizer. A person could earn a living digging, shucking, preparing and packing shellfish, but it was hard work. At the turn of the century, a barrel's worth of clams (about a dozen to a dozen and a half bushels of harvested clams) would fetch a worker about three dollars. A good worker could fill about a barrel and a half a week, so his weekly pay would amount to about four dollars and fifty cents!

• • •

During the early to mid-1800s, Truro prospered as fishing brought the town to life. Pamet River Harbor became a busy port and a wharf business grew to new heights, pointing to the successes from the sea. The Union Wharf was constructed in 1829 and the following year a shipyard was established, producing schooners and brigs. Fish packing buildings, sail lofts and salt vats completed the scene. Also built during this growth phase was the Union Company Store specializing in ship chandler. The tide was to turn as the result of a series of failures beginning with the great gale of October 1841. During that storm, the town lost ten percent of its seamen. The store, which reflected her earlier successes, now mirrored the town's collapse as it went out of business in 1860.

• • •

The first whalers of Cape Cod were the Native Indians who went out into Cape Cod Bay to harpoon the leviathan. Early settlers from Sandwich to Provincetown would rejoice at the sight of a whale washed up along their shore. They also went out in boats to hunt the whales that in those days populated the Cape waters. In later years, crews had to venture further to find whales, their journeys eventually taking them as far away as Africa and the Pacific. In 1760, Provincetown had a fleet of a dozen whaling ships. During the nineteenth century the fleet attracted whaling men from the Azores, Canary Islands and Cape Verde Islands to work on Provincetown whaling vessels. Wellfleet also had a number of whaling vessels, and there are some that claim "Wellfleet" evolved from the name "Whale Fleet."

• • •

In the days prior to the railroad Cape Cod was connected to Boston, New York and New Bedford via a fleet of packets. The first packets began making their runs during the early eighteenth century, carrying upwards of fifty passengers, mail, crops and fish products to Boston and carrying back goods Cape Codders required. By the early nineteenth century the packet was a necessity with most towns along the Cape boasting their own speedy vessel. To keep things interesting races were held between the packets to see who had the fastest ship on the peninsula. The trip to Boston took six hours and a round trip ticket was about a dollar and a half. The coming of the railroad to Cape Cod in the mid-nineteenth century put an end to the packet business.

• • •

Dennis has long been associated with the sea. Dennisport produced a large and profitable fishing fleet, West Dennis produced more ship captains than any other Dennis village, and East Dennis produced large sailing ships at its Sesuit Harbor shipyards. Begun in 1849 by the three brothers Shiverick (Asa, Paul and David) along with sea captain Christopher Hall, Shiverick Shipyards produced eight clipper ships and a number of schooners during its decade and a half in operation.

The first clipper was launched in 1850 and was aptly named *Revenue*. At 546 tons she would be the smallest clipper of the lot. Following her was *Hippogriffe*, in 1852, at 156 feet long and 678 tons. In 1858, with Captain Anthony Howes of East Dennis in command, she struck a reef in the Java Sea. Fortunately, the damaged vessel was able to make Hong Kong. The reef would forever be known as Hippogriffe Rock.

The 1,000-ton, 170-foot *Belle of the West* would be the third clipper built at the Shiverick Yard. Launched in 1853, she ran the East India trade route for fifteen years before sinking with a cargo of rice. Next came *Kit Carson* in 1854 at 1,016 tons. Owned by successful East Dennis sea captain and ship owner Prince S. Crowell, *Kit Carson* would become a casualty of war off the coast of Brazil in the 1860s.

Wild Hunter, christened in 1855 as the fifth Shiverick clipper, was a 1,081-ton workhorse commanded by legendary East Dennis sea captain Joshua Sears who was known for his speed records. The next year *Webfoot* was launched. At 1,091 tons she would become the largest of the vessels built at the Sesuit shipyards. Though she was fast, she was also prone to accident. She was heavily damaged in 1858 as Captain Milton Hedge attempted to round Cape Horn. After running aground off France in 1864 she was sold. Repaired, *Webfoot* sailed for the next twenty-two years before being lost off Canada in 1886.

The seventh clipper was the 648-ton *Christopher Hall*, launched in 1858 and named for the sea captain himself who died the previous year. In 1867 she struck a reef in the South Pacific and sank. *Ellen Sears* would be the final clipper built. Launched in 1863, she was lost in the Pacific four years later.

• • •

The great thing about Cape Cod of old is that one thing fed off another. Sail lofts fed off the successful packet business, coopers fed off the successful cranberry industry. The success of one business brought growth to a dozen others. One Cape line of business to actually feed off failure was the wrecking business. With the large number of shipwrecks along the Cape's outer shores, experienced wreckers were needed to salvage the cargoes of the wrecked vessels and, if possible, save the vessel as well. During the early years, a grounded ship going to pieces on the shore was fair game. But as potential profits, and potential losses, grew more substantial toward the end of the nineteenth century, the need for experienced wrecking crews was great. Their efforts saved many an otherwise doomed vessel and her cargo from the ocean graveyard.

• • •

During the early settlement of the Cape there was a great need for good local tanners to produce leather products from animal hides. Like the blacksmith, the tanner became a necessary craftsman for a community. As time went on, the local tanner gave way to more mechanized methods and larger factories. In the mid-1800s, Edward Clark opened a tannery in Eastham, erecting a three-story building and employing about two dozen locals. The process included soaking the hides in vats and then rubbing the leather with fish oils. Sometimes the leather would be dyed. The tannery at Eastham produced leather bags, shoes and items used in daily life. It remained in business for about fifteen years and closed because mechanized competition could do the job cheaper and faster.

• • •

Swamplands were good for two things on old Cape Cod: cranberries and iron. Early settlers of Bourne and neighboring Wareham discovered the bogs and swamplands wept with iron. Although it was by no means top quality ore, the people of Bourne set to work harvesting the rust colored mineral from the wetlands. Foundries were established during the mid-nineteenth century, notably the Pocasset Iron Company and the Howard Foundry Company, which produced kettles, plates and nails. The Tremont Nail Company of Wareham began as the Tremont Iron Company back in 1845.

• • •

Located in Sandwich, in what is now Sagamore, was Keith and Ryder, also known as the Keith Car and Manufacturing Company, which produced the vehicles that helped America expand westward. Started in 1826, the company employed hundreds of Cape Codders to manufacture stagecoaches, prairie schooners, wagons, ox carts, buggies and railroad freight cars. The company was in business for a little more than one hundred years and closed its factories toward the end of the 1920s with the coming of the Great Depression.

Scales into Pearls and an Elixir for the Ages

Cape Cod has produced a surprising number of people whose ideas contributed to new ways of getting things done. Call them inventors, or entrepreneurs, or even opportunists, this area has never lacked individuals who had an interest in building a better mousetrap and making a profit at the same time.

Many enterprises were started on Cape Cod, each the brainchild of practical men and women who had a nose for innovation. Most of these ideas and businesses never had an impact further than the villages of their origin, but several graduated beyond the Cape to have national importance.

Gustavus Swift, for example, whose roots went back to nineteenth century Sandwich, eventually took his skills at bartering livestock to Chicago and founded Swift and Company, one of the great meat packing companies of the country.

In the early nineteenth century the Winslow family of Brewster built a fulling mill in the west section of town that is said to have produced the first factory-made woolen cloth in America. The factory model was copied and transferred to other New England mill sites.

Caleb Chase of West Harwich decided not to follow his many brothers to sea and, instead, concentrated on the emerging coffee importation business, developing a fortune as a partner in the well-known Chase and Sanborn "coffee empire." Still another Cape Codder, Samuel Mayo Nickerson, left his native Chatham and carried his financial skills to the mid-west, becoming president of the First National Bank of Chicago.

These examples of creative Cape Codders who played on the wider national stage were paralleled by hundreds of individuals whose ideas had local, if often only temporary, impact.

The short-lived Provincetown skunk farm of the late nineteenth century, an enterprise that produced skunks for both meat and fur, selling the pelts for between four and six dollars apiece, was such an example. Falmouth's early twentieth century attempt to become the mushroom growing capital of the nation was ended when the Gifford Street operation was wiped out by a persistent blight that closed the business after only a few years.

Perhaps typical of the kinds of inventive activity and entrepre-neurial spirit associated with business that went on in Cape towns is the example of Harwich. In the mid-nineteenth century the town boasted a soap factory, a tanning business, and a plant for the manufacturing of fishermen's boots and men's and ladies' slippers. A barrel factory was constructed to serve the needs of the growing cranberry industry in the town and there was a shirt and overall factory built in 1865 that employed as many as two hundred and fifty people. A cotton and woolen factory, a boiler plant, and a tap and die factory were also part of Harwich's nineteenth century industrial past.

In every Cape Cod town there were people who seized upon an idea with the intention of making both an improvement in a process or product and, hopefully, a lot of money.

Mabel Kimball Baker started the Colonial Candle Company in her Hyannis kitchen by making traditional hand-dipped candles from the bayberry bushes that are found throughout the Cape. She began her enterprise by selling candles from the porch of her house. In 1910, she received a small order from a Boston retail company that was given a sample of her candles by a summer visitor. The product sold well and the initial order was repeated and increased.

Sensing that she struck on something, she and her husband, Walter D. Baker, pooled their resources and built a factory in Hyannis to mass-produce the popular candles. By the 1920s, the candle company was selling millions of candles throughout the nation. Today the company continues to hold a strong share of the candle market from its Main Street, Hyannis headquarters.

Another Hyannis inventor and entrepreneur was Mr. Edward Petow who developed an unusual process of using herring scales to provide the luster for artificial pearls. Founding the Cape Cod United Products Company during the period of the First World War, Mr. Petow rented the old Hyannis Yacht Club building on Pleasant Street and began experimenting with chemicals that would bind the scale to the glass beads that were used as the pearls. The actual processing of the herring scale involved putting them into vats where a secret chemical process reduced them in several hours to a silvery liquid.

The glass beads were then dipped in the liquid to acquire the sheen that made them unique and highly prized. Calling his herring scale concoction "Essence D'Orient," Mr. Petow eventually secured the rights to herring runs up and down the New England coast. At one time the company was purchasing thousands of pounds of herring scale for its operation. Locally, the pearls were marketed as "Priscilla Pearls" and they were very successful. It was said that the finished product was indistinguishable from the real thing and only the best experts and chemical analysis could detect it from the genuine pearl. The business thrived until overseas competition and the eventual depressed economy of the 1930s ended production.

One of the more interesting inventions credited to a Cape Codder revolves around what was called "Castoria." This antecedent to a steady stream of homeopathic medical remedies came out of the barn of Doctor Samuel Pitcher of Hyannis. As with most inventors, his product contained a secret formula that was said to be based on the sassafras root combined with a healthy dose of alcohol. The product was marketed as a cure for such nineteenth century problems as dyspepsia, dropsy, dysentery, and "summer complaints."

The reputation of Doctor Pitcher's product began to grow locally and eventually attracted the attention of Mr. Charles Fletcher of New York City. Fletcher Brothers was a well-known name in the types of herbal medicines that were being sold around the northeast at that time. In 1869, Pitcher sold his Castoria formula to Fletcher's company for ten thousand dollars. Within a very short time, Fletcher Brothers created one of the longest marketed and largest selling health remedies in American history. Under the slogan "Children cry for it," Fletcher's Castoria became the most popular elixir sold anywhere in the country.

Clearly though, not every invention produced and operated by Cape Codders was a success. Valentine Doane Jr. of Harwich patented a baby carriage in the 1880s that never caught the public's attention. Joseph Cummings and William Howes operated a clothing manufacturing business in Orleans that produced Plymouth Rock Pants. Unfortunately, the pants never became as well-known as the famous rock and the business failed.

Even the promising "Queen Anne Commode," produced by the Harwichport Manufacturing Company in the late nineteenth century, did not achieve much of a following.

One thing is still certain. Today's entrepreneurs learned that a product that carries the name of Cape Cod attached to it generally has a good chance to sell. Cape Codders continue to create and exploit new markets, proving that the inventive spirit remains very much with us still.

Haymaking from Salt Marshes

Our Cape Cod ancestors from centuries ago utilized the lands and the seas to form their very existence. They eagerly accepted what the Cape had to offer. In those days nothing was wasted, everything had value.

For instance, Cape Codders harvested seaweed from the beaches during the late summer and fall to "bank up," or insulate, around the foundations of their homes against the frigid winter winds to come.

The soil being so poor for farming, the Cape farm folk did their best to feed their families. What was not plantable soil was either too sandy to support crops or else bog-like. Yet they triumphed on this playing field as well, utilizing the bogs and sands to cultivate cranberries. It seemed no matter what the conditions, Cape Codders found a way to turn what would typically be defeat into a victory.

Even a shipwreck was a bountiful harvest for those who lived on the Lower Cape. Cast ashore at night in a gale, within days the wrecked vessel would be stripped of its cargo, its masts, spars, sails, navigational equipment, even its planking to build barns and chicken houses. Such wrecked vessels would be devoured by the local townsfolk, taking what they needed from the sea's offering.

Cape "mooncussers" actually lured unsuspecting ships into the shoals by walking with a lit lantern over the dunes in order to resemble a ship successfully navigating the waters closer to shore. These mooncussers did their best work on dark, moonless nights when sailors had to feel their way along the coastline in the pitch. Though much has been made of this dark occupation, it was not as common as the old stories depict. On the whole, Cape Codders did their best to prevent shipwrecks for who knew for sure whose own son or husband or father was aboard yonder vessel rising and falling with the mounting waves.

But for those who farmed and owned livestock, earning their living from the soil rather than from the sea, a certain feature of the Cape played an important role in their day to day agrarian exist- ence. Livestock required hay for fodder and bedding. As the crop yield from Cape soil was much less than what farmers were used to harvesting inland, therefore requiring more land to produce the same yield, it was impractical use of the land to devote much of it to the cultivation of hay. The Cape environment, though, provided a natural solution to satisfy this need.

Salt marshes, like Great Marsh running along the northern edges of West Barnstable, yielded vast amounts of salt hay. This salt hay, though somewhat inferior to regular hay in terms of nutritional content and taste, provided adequate fodder and bedding for the Cape's livestock.

Native Indians of the area called the tidal marshes Moskeehtuckqut. The very earliest settlers quickly realized the value of Barnstable's marshlands, one of the largest tidal marshes on the Massachusetts coastline, some eight thousand acres in area, four miles of salt hay!

Though settlement began in the eastern part of Barnstable near the harbor, then called Mattakeese, a number of families from Scituate relocated to what was then called the settlement of Great Marshes, now known as the village of West Barnstable. The soil at Great Marshes, just south of the hay grounds, was considered to be some of the richest on the peninsula. And the marshes provided all the hay they would ever need.

At first, the salt marshes were available to the local farmers of the area on the rather informal basis known as common owner- ship. A farmer and his farm hands merely went to the marshlands and took what they needed. But soon, as the population grew and the number of farmers demanding hay expanded, the towns found the need to divide up the salt marshes and draw up legal rights of ownership. Much bickering commenced over these valuable lands as the ownership of salt marsh acreage became both important to farmers and profitable to those who went into the business of selling hay to farmers.

Inland, the cultivation of hay during June and July was a rather scientific process. Different factors, such as optimizing the harvest to produce the greatest yield while maintaining maximum nutritional content of the hay, maximum digestibility and maximum state of curing, all had to be considered.

In the salt marshes of the Cape a different scientific process was employed - the hay was harvested during the lowest possible tides in the month of August, plain and simple.

Harvested salt hay would be piled on staddles - platforms built of planks atop posts planted into the marsh - in order to keep the reaped grasses dry above the tidal seawater. Such a harvest as this was truly a race against time. It was a race against the tides, a race against bad weather, and a race against the nasty green head flies that frequented the marshes during the heat of August.

The only way a farmer could harvest hay in a tidal marsh was to employ the use of such staddles and to pray that unusually high seas or a sudden storm did not ruin the crop until it could be moved to the family farm. The great salt marshes of Barnstable contained thousands of staddles elevating the salt hay harvest of an entire town above the damaging waters of high tide.

Haymaking from salt marshes petered out during the latter years of the nineteenth century. The Cape population's diet was being provided more and more by off-Cape farmers as the railroad firmly connected Cape Cod to the mainland. Left to the elements, the staddles fell to the hundreds of storms over the past century. Today the salt marshes are quiet places, their vegetation gently swaying in the meandering breezes.

Cranberries Color the Cape

Vaccinium macrocarpon, that is the scientific name for the American cranberry, a native fruit with more than one hundred varieties.

It is Massachusetts' state berry. Here on the Cape we are familiar with two varieties: the Early Black, which is blackish-red in color and matures in September, and the Later Howes, which is larger yet lighter in color and matures in early October.

Though cranberries grow in other parts of the world, the American cranberry is considered the largest, the tastiest and the most versatile. Of the states across the country where cranberries grow, Massachusetts has consistently been the largest single producer of the native berry with two million barrels harvested annually at a value of $100 million. More than 13,000 acres of Massachusetts' lands are dedicated to growing cranberries, including many, many acres on Cape Cod. An additional 50,000 acres of natural wetlands support these bogs.

Like most things native to this country, the Native Indians were the first to enjoy the cranberry. They picked the berries, which they called sassamanesh, and ate them raw. They also cooked them, creating sauces and preserves or even mixed their cranberries with venison to make pemmican, rich in protein and providing much needed vitamins, especially Vitamin C, during the long winter months.

Explorer Robert Peary understood the value of the tart fruit and brought a supply of pemmican with him on his journey to the North Pole. The Native Indians of the Cape and southeastern Massachusetts also used cranberries as a dye as well as for medicinal purposes.

The earliest settlers realized their value. Besides eating them raw, they boiled them with sugar to create a sauce or sometimes sweetened them with maple syrup. The native cranberry was even once used to appease the King of England. In 1677, Charles II was upset when he learned that the colonists minted pine tree shillings without his permission. As a token of apology, the colonists sent the King, among other items, three thousand codfish, two hogshead of corn and ten barrels of cranberries.

One of three fruits native to North America, the other two being the Concord grape and the blueberry, the cranberry grows on low-lying vines in acid-peat, bog-like soil. Most successful conditions include sand mixed with the peat soil as well as an ample supply

Late September brings the cranberry harvest, as shown in this old postcard. (J. Coogan Collection)

of fresh water. The plants need to be sanded every three to four years to help aerate the soil and flooded to a depth of several inches above the vines from December to April in order to protect them against frost and insects.

Many elements concerning the early days of cranberry cultivation are relegated to the realm of speculation. For instance, the very name "cranberry" seems to have a number of roots. Some say the name comes from the English "craneberry" because the stamens of the plant resemble the beak of a crane. Some say it is because the bogs attracted cranes, although cranes themselves do not eat cranberries. Others say the name derives from the German "kraanbere" (kraan translates as crane). Still others say it is from the Dutch "kranebere" (same translation).

Though the Native Indians and the early settlers made the cranberry part of their diet, both groups picked the berries where they found them growing. Throughout the seventeenth and eighteenth centuries this relationship with the cranberry continued in the same fashion as no one actually considered cultivating the berry. The vines grew in swampy bogs - inexpensive lands considered to have no worth. Yet this was about to change.

Most accounts point to the men of Dennis and Harwich as those who experimented with the cranberry during the early to mid-nineteenth century and created the industry that still thrives today. Henry Hall of Dennis noticed in 1816 that cranberry vines in a bog on his farm actually yielded more fruit when sand blew onto the plants. In his bog he conducted experiments to determine the best conditions for growing the berries. As his bog began to grow, his brother Isaiah Hall got into the act. He operated a cooperage and his services provided barrels for the harvest. In fact, his barrel is still the official unit of measure used today.

Dennis may be where cranberry cultivation was born, but Harwich was where it grew into a major Massachusetts industry. In 1847, Cyrus Cahoon planted what is considered the first commercial bog on a quarter acre of his land. His neighbors did not think that people would actually pay money for a berry they could easily go out and pick for themselves. A few years later, when Cahoon's bog was yielding a healthy crop, and when he found a market for his berries, his neighbors realized they were wrong. Others began to clear their bogs and plant vines in the wake of Cahoon's success.

Though ridiculed, Captain Abiathar Doane of Harwich experimented with setting his vines close together and discovered that it increased the yield in his bog. The experiments of Abel D. Makepeace of West Barnstable developed a superior berry, making him the world's largest cranberry producer and earning him the title "Cranberry King."

Little by little, the pioneers of the industry were finding out what made cranberry vines happy. The happier the vines, the greater the yield, the larger the berries and the tastier the fruit. It was trial by error much of the time, but slowly the secrets of the cranberry began to unravel. The growers of Massachusetts now knew more about cranberries than anyone else in the world. Their craft was both a science and an art.

A bog would normally begin to produce berries just three years after its creation. Given proper care, a bog could continue to produce berries indefinitely. It is not uncommon to find century old bogs still in operation today. The work was hard yet a typical bog owner could make a decent living. It is believed that just one acre of bog could support an average nineteenth century Cape Cod family. A few acres could make its owner rather well off.

It is a well-known fact that a good cranberry bounces. John "Peg-Leg" Webb discovered this characteristic of the berry when he accidentally dropped a large number of cranberries in his barn and noticed that some bounced on the wooden floorboards and others did not. Examining the berries, he realized that the ones that did not bounce were inferior or spoiled.

Cranberry separators were later developed to test the berries for their "bounceabilty." A berry was given seven chances to bounce over four-inch high hurdles. If they failed the test they were discarded. High-grade berries were those that bounced over the very first hurdles. These berries would be sold as fresh fruit. Medium grade berries took more than a couple of attempts to clear the separator hurdles and would end up in juice drinks and sauces.

A good berry also floats. This is because a cranberry has four air pockets, an important characteristic when wet harvesting methods were later employed.

Cranberries were picked by hand up until the late-1800s when wooden scoops were first introduced. Picking time prior to the advent of wooden scoops was as much a social event as a job. In some areas, whole communities would gather at the local bogs in September to harvest the annual crop. In family owned bogs, the children would miss school during the harvest season. Some communities actually began school in October after the harvest.

Pickers would gather at the bog with their measures in hand. A measure was a six-quart pail made of tin into which the picker would place his or her cranberries. The bog would be segregated into a series of four-foot wide rows cordoned off with fishing line or rope. Two pickers would work side by side in each row. Behind them would walk a person who checked their progress and made sure that the vines in their wake were truly picked clean.

"Coming ashore," as it was called, referred to the point when the picker's measure became full and was then brought forth from the bog to the screen and barrels where the good berries would be separated by hand from the bad. A tally keeper would give the picker credit for six quarts. The small, unusable berries would fall through the screen; good berries would be packed in barrels and then placed in wagons for transport to the buyer. At the end of the harvest, the bog owner would tally up the number of quarts harvested by each picker. For the longest time the going rate was one and a half cents per quart.

Toward the turn of the century the tools of the trade became more "sophisticated" in order to cater to the growers' needs. Actual growers who knew best what was needed to do the job developed these tools. For instance, a curved-bottom rocker scoop replaced the original flat-bottom tip up scoop. The curved bottom allowed the picker to make a number of consecutive passes through the vines without emptying the scoop after each pass. Other scoops were made for tender, young vines while long handled picking rakes were used for snagging berries at the edges of the bog.

Portuguese and Finnish immigrants arriving on Cape Cod found work in the bogs. These hardworking immigrants built many of the bogs that helped to grow the industry. Some were hired as migrant workers, employed during key times during the year, especially at harvest time. Others went on to own their own bogs. The work was tough, the risk was great, and the return was not so great. Disease or frost could destroy a crop. Climate could hamper the year's harvest. Yet the growers persevered and the industry continued to grow.

During the days of handpicking a good picker could harvest fifteen barrels a day - some 1,500 pounds worth. As mechanized methods were developed that figure jumped to seventy-five barrels. Wooden hand scoops were used into the 1950s; for one hundred years the industry changed very little as one still had to get down on hands and knees to harvest the berries.

With the invention of self-propelled machines one person could do the work of many, harvesting about 10,000 pounds of cranberries daily. Yield grew substantially. A half million barrel annual crop in the 1930s tripled to one and a half million barrels by the 1960s. As yield grew, researchers developed new uses for the berry such as the cranberry juice cocktail. As new uses were developed and markets grew, more cranberries were needed to keep up with demand. Today's harvest is nearly five million barrels annually; about 200 billion berries. Half of those cranberries are harvested from Massachusetts' bogs.

Wet harvesting was developed in Wisconsin in the 1950s and began to be regularly employed in Massachusetts during the 1960s. The bogs would be flooded to a few inches above the vines. Vehicles with balloon tires so not to crush the plants and with a waterwheel churning the waters into turbulence would move over the bog. The waterwheel, called an eggbeater, would not make contact with the vines, but the turbulence in the water would cause the buoyant berries to separate from their vines and rise to the surface.

The berries would then be pushed with a boom to one side of the bog where trucks stood by to take the harvested crop. Wet harvesting is faster and more economical than dry harvesting, and also inflicts less damage on the vines. About seventy-five percent of the cranberries in Massachusetts are wet harvested and are used for sauces, jellies and drinks. The rest are dry harvested and are sold as fresh fruit.

Today, bogs provide a natural habitat for wildlife as well as for plant life. They also provide us with an ever-changing vista as the bogs show a different face for each of the four seasons. Winter's coat of dull reddish-brown gives way to a blanket of small pink flower blossoms by late spring. Light green berries begin to appear in the summer and grow until fall when the berries mature, becoming bright red and ready for harvest.

And then the cycle begins anew, nature picking up where she left off, on and on, year after year. One hundred years from now cranberries will continue to grow on Cape Cod ... and Cape Codders will continue to harvest them.

Harnessing the Cape Winds

There is something almost nautical about windmills, especially here on Cape Cod with her salt air breezes.

During the eighteenth and nineteenth centuries the Cape was

Old Higgins Farm windmill, built in 1795. (J. Sheedy photo)

home to some fifty or so windmills. Each town along this narrow land had its handful. The remaining windmills, scattered here and there across the Cape, today resemble sailing ships hard aground, their four mighty arms pointing toward four equally opposite corners of the universe, their gray weathered shingles staring like thousands of eyes at a modern day world spinning round and round.

For many years these titans stood upon the landscape. Now they seem to be passing their retirement years, watching us as we hurry along our way down Route 6A in Brewster or Route 6 in Eastham. They stand as proud reminders of a more agrarian time, their naked arms now still, silent, their working days through.

Imagine Cape Cod three hundred and fifty years ago. There existed pockets of settlements here and there in Sandwich, Barnstable, Yarmouth, Eastham, groups of families huddling together in a vast windswept wilderness some thirty or forty miles out to sea. They hunted and fished for their meals and grew vegetables and grains. The Native Indians of the area introduced these early settlers to the ways of growing the native crops, in particular this stony soil's most successful grain - corn, the staple of early Massachusetts and Cape Cod life.

With grains holding such an important place in the early settlers' diet, it seems only natural that windmills would dot the rolling Cape Cod landscape. Mills required the talents of three individuals. First, of course, was the millwright who normally built on high ground where the strongest winds could be found. Next came the millstone picker who carved the millstone out of granite and maintained its upkeep. And last was the miller himself, many times a retired sea captain as such a person was used to working with wind and canvas.

Maintaining the mill was an important function of the miller. Machinery needed to be kept in peak working order and lubricated in order to avoid the risk of fire. The windmill was, in many cases, a popular spot for townsfolk to congregate as they collected

The Jonathan Young Windmill at Town Cove in Orleans dates to the early eighteenth century. (J. Sheedy photo)

their grains and caught up on the latest village news.

Within two decades after the arrival of the Pilgrims the arms were turning and the millstones of Cape Cod were grinding away. Benjamin Nye was one of Sandwich's earliest settlers. In 1669 he built a gristmill on what is now known as Nye Pond, becoming only the second such mill on Cape at the time. In later years he built a fulling mill as well. Fellow Sandwich resident Thomas Dexter had earlier built the town's first gristmill in 1654. Up to that time Sandwich residents had to travel all the way to Plymouth to have their corn ground.

The first windmill actually constructed on Cape Cod was at Cobb's Hill in Barnstable village. Built in 1687 by millwright Thomas Paine of Eastham, it was an eight-sided smock-type mill. Paine received £32 for his efforts. This Barnstable village mill was joined by another, built in 1785 at Jail Lane. By the turn of the seventeenth century the town boasted three windmills, the third being Uncle Owen Bacon's mill at the corner of South and Sea streets in Hyannis. At that time, Cape Cod had nearly forty windmills grinding grain across the peninsula.

The Jonathan Young Mill, originally built in 1710 at South Orleans, was purchased by Captain Henry Hunt and relocated via Nantucket Sound to his Hyannisport farm in 1897. The "Captain Hunt Mill" remained in operation into the early years of the twentieth century, and in 1983 was on the move again, back to its native Lower Cape town where it now resides at Town Cove.

The Judah Baker Windmill along Bass River in South Yarmouth was constructed in 1791. Originally a Dennis mill, it was moved at least once within the town before being relocated across the river in 1863 to its current spot guarding the entrance to Bass River. It remained in operation grinding grain until 1891 when its services were no longer in demand.

Along Route 6A in Brewster is the smock-type Old Higgins Farm Windmill. Set back upon the acres of gently rolling terrain, it has views of Cape Cod Bay across the marshes to the north. Built in 1795, it was moved to its present location from Ellis Landing in 1974. It ceased operation around the turn of the twentieth century as did many of the Cape windmills as grains became more easily purchased from the local store, the heartland of the country now in full swing.

Chatham seems as if sprinkled with small windmills. Standing upon one end of Chase Park in the village center is the 1797 Godfrey Mill. For one hundred and one years it ground corn for the community. It remained on as a landmark, grinding only on special occasions. Two storms, one in 1907 and another in 1929, did much damage to the mill, causing its shutdown. In 1956 the town was given a gift of the mill and it was moved to its present location about a half mile or so from its previous location on Stage Harbor Road.

Along Route 6 in Eastham is the Old Mill of Eastham resting upon the village green. Built in Plymouth during the late 1600s, it was shipped across the bay to the Cape in the late 1700s and stood in Truro for a number of years before its final move to Eastham in 1793. It is now the oldest operating mill on Cape.

The smock-type Old East Windmill at Heritage Plantation started out as an Orleans windmill. Around 1800 it was built utilizing extra timbers left after renovations were made to the Old Congregational Meetinghouse. The mill was moved in 1819 from Snows Hill to a spot near Meeting House Pond. By 1889, the mill was closed. In the 1950s it was moved within Orleans and in 1968 was moved again to Heritage Plantation where a motor was installed to turn the arms and grind corn for museum visitors to view.

Bourne is home to three windmills. Two are owned privately, the third rests beside the Aptucxet Trading Post. Known as the Jefferson Windmill, it once belonged to nineteenth century actor and Bourne resident Joseph Jefferson.

Brewster's Factory Village

A drive through Brewster today doesn't give any hint that the town was once one of the early industrial leaders of Cape Cod. Today, Brewster lists only 5.4 percent of its employment in the area of manufacturing but in its earliest years of settlement, this bayside town was known for its west end factory center in the Stony Brook valley.

Soon after the spread of settlement beyond Plymouth began to bring people to Cape Cod, the potential for using the strong flowing waters of what was then called Saquatucket Brook was recognized. The area was well inhabited for centuries by native peoples and early European settlers called the lands below the Mill Ponds "Indian Fields" because this is where indigenous people cleared the land for planting. All of the land in this period of time was part of the Town of Yarmouth. Thomas Prence was given permission around 1662 to purchase land in the area of the stream where he built the first water-powered gristmill.

Before the end of the seventeenth century, Kenelm Winslow set up a fulling mill on the stream. The history of the Winslow family is so much a part of the area that for some time the brook was referred to by local residents as Winslow's Brook. The fulling process was used in producing woolen cloth. The water from the brook was channeled through a sluice gate to a mill wheel where paddles pounded the water-soaked homespun cloth, making the weave tighter and smoother. So-called "fuller's earth," a type of clay, was added to the wool to soften it. To further reduce the oil content of the cloth, crushed leaves of the common soapwort plant were added to the water.

With the growth of the mill complex along the brook, it became necessary to engineer a means of holding the water in Lower Mill Pond so that it could be used on demand by the industries as needed. A millrace and flume was constructed so that water could be moved to turn the various wheels that connected with it.

Throughout the seventeenth and eighteenth centuries, activity around the small brook increased along with the population of the west section of the town. But it was the nineteenth century that saw the greatest expansion of manufacturing sites. Another woolen mill was constructed at the conclusion of the War of 1812. It was said to be the first mill to produce factory-made woolen cloth in the United States. A cotton mill and a wool carding mill, as well as a facility for making paper, were added to the factory complex by the 1820s.

In 1830 another Winslow family member, William, built a tannery that supplied leather for many of the small shoemaking establishments on Cape Cod. As part of the process, Hemlock bark was brought in from Maine to help cure the leather. The growing salt industry of the town supplied enough salt to assist in the leather softening process.

There were other small industries that developed in what came to be known as Brewster's "factory village." There was a stove and tin plate business run by Bartlett B. Winslow which started in 1854. He later combined this enterprise with a substantial grocery business that continued almost until the end of the century.

There were cabinetmakers and a knitting factory within a mile of the brook. Josef Berger, in his book *Cape Cod Pilot*, claims that Sidney Winslow started a shoemaking factory near the mill sites that eventually outgrew its Brewster location, moving inland to Brockton where it became the mighty United Shoe Machinery Company. Winslow became a wealthy man because of this business and eventually settled in neighboring Orleans where he enjoyed a well-heeled retirement.

Corn grinding occupied much of the stream activity during the latter part of the nineteenth century and the building that is now referred to as "the old mill" was built in 1873 for this purpose. The structure replaced another mill that burned in the spring of 1871. Some of the beams used in the construction came from the once extensive salt works that were located near Cape Cod Bay around Wing's Island.

During its lifetime, the present mill building has seen a variety of uses including the grinding of corn meal, but it has also served as an overall factory and an ice creamery. In 1940 the town purchased the historic structure along with its adjacent herring run and the site has been preserved as a working museum and natural history exhibit. Today, a visitor is more apt to visit the site for the annual spring run of alewives than to look for evidence of a long ago business activity.

Boston and Sandwich Glass Works

In 1824, Deming Jarves, a Bostonian involved in the glass making business, came south to Sandwich for a vacation of hunting and fishing. The previous year his father died, leaving him with money and the family business. After a period of malaise, Jarves was awakening to the challenges facing him as he considered his dream of revolutionizing the glass making industry.

While he was on vacation in Sandwich, Jarves noticed the sandy beaches and the thick woodlands. He began to consider the notion of building a glass factory in this Cape Cod setting where the sand to make the glass was to be found in vast quantities and the trees to fuel the furnaces grew all around. The next year, in July 1825, Deming Jarves opened his Boston and Sandwich Glass Works at Factory and Harbor streets.

It turned out that the Sandwich sand was not the right kind for glass making. It contained too much iron. No matter, Jarves shipped in sand from as far away as New Jersey and Florida. Up went housing for the workers and the chimneys of the factory pumped black smoke into the skies. The glass factory was up and running.

The company met with instant success. Sales tripled in the short span of four years, from $32,000 in 1827 to $93,000 in 1830. The operation was a boon to the Sandwich economy, employing some five hundred people in 1850 and creating a number of spin-off jobs. A lumber company was established to cut the trees in a 2,000-acre forest to feed the fires. A transportation system was put into place. Housing was built around the factory for the skilled workers being relocated to Sandwich. Jarves even had his own steamship built, the *Acorn*, because he was fed up with the railroad's fees. Soon the company was producing a half-ton of glassware each week, $600,000 worth of glassware per year.

Jarves was truly ahead of his time, producing the country's first pressed and laced glass. Besides producing artistic glassware, he also produced basic glassware products that were affordable and could be used by the average person in their daily life. Tumblers, plates, salt shakers, lamps, bowls, candleholders - the use of automation and molds making the glassware affordable. Yet, at the same time the company created some of the most exquisite pieces in the world and experimented with different shades of color to create works of art unmatched anywhere. Jarves covered both ends of the

A fine nineteenth century woodcut depicting the factories of Sandwich Glass Works in operation. (J. Coogan Collection)

spectrum, from the artistic to the practical. He became the king of the glass world, revolutionizing the craft as he hoped he would.

In the short span of a quarter century Sandwich became the most successful town on Cape. After thirty-three years with the company, Jarves resigned to start another glass company that he planned to hand down to his son, John, who worked along with him. Opened in 1864, the septuagenarian Jarves' new venture was called Cape Cod Glass Works. Sadly, though, his son died and Jarves lost the will to pursue this latest dream. Within five years he too was dead.

Boston and Sandwich Glass continued on without its founder. With the Civil War behind them, the glassmakers of Sandwich looked forward to the prosperity to follow. Prosperous times did follow the company into the 1880s, but a series of events sounded the death knell. First, in 1884, the town of Sandwich split up. The villages of Bourne, Buzzards Bay, Cataumet, Pocasset, Sagamore and Monument Beach became the town of Bourne. The tax base of the town was essentially cut in half with the division. Sandwich lost much of its usable coastline as well. Successful companies, such as Keith and Ryder who made stagecoaches and freight cars, were now located in Sagamore instead of in Sandwich, and with them went their tax dollars.

Meanwhile, competition sprang up out in the mid-west in the form of other glassmakers producing affordable glassware. Their furnaces were fired by less expensive and inexhaustible natural gas rather than by wood ... wood that was now being shipped to Sandwich from elsewhere as all the forests in town were gone, cut down to warm homes and fire the factory furnaces. Other east coast glass companies were making the move out west, but Boston and Sandwich hesitated.

A strike resulting from a wage dispute at the factory finished off the glass works for good. Once work ground to a halt and the furnaces went cold they were never fired up again. A number of attempts to reopen the factory failed and Sandwich, suffering from massive unemployment, fell into a great depression. The closing of the glass works crippled the town, sending out a ripple effect thus devastating other businesses in the town. It took many decades for Sandwich to recover.

In its more than sixty-year run, Boston and Sandwich Glass Works produced about $30 million worth of glass. Its products found their way into homes across the country and to every foreign port where America's ships sailed. Today, Sandwich glass can be found in museums and in antiques shops. One such museum is the Sandwich Glass Museum where the history of the company and its beautiful artistry are kept alive.

Provincetown's Place in Whaling History

Nantucket and New Bedford are perhaps the most well-known American whaling ports. Beginning in the early nineteenth century and extending to the advent of the twentieth century, the pursuit of the whale dominated the economy of these two Massachusetts towns.

What may be less known is the fact that Provincetown was an equally important whaling center and its connection with whaling began earlier and lasted longer than either of its two more famous competitors.

Even before the American Revolution, Provincetown men were engaged in offshore whaling. In one early eighteenth century newspaper there is a reference to a dozen whaling vessels that were calling the Cape-tip their homeport.

Interest in whaling was acquired from the native people who greeted the Pilgrims in 1620. The value of whales as a commodity was part of the seventeenth century economic life of Cape Cod. In 1690, Icabod Paddock of Yarmouth went to Nantucket to teach the islanders the art of killing whales.

Provincetown, by its location and fine harbor, quickly became a departure point for ships headed for the Atlantic whaling grounds. Eventually, the town became the permanent home for these whaling men. In 1776 there were forty vessels of more than one hundred tons registered in Barnstable County as whaling ships. The bulk of these were from Provincetown. But it was the nineteenth century that saw Provincetown come into its own as a major whaling port. As perhaps the leading fishing center in Massachusetts, the connection to whaling as another seagoing occupation was a natural choice for many Cape-tip men. The market for oil and bone grew through the century. By the time of the Civil War there were more than sixty registered whaling ships that sailed from Provincetown.

For much of this period Provincetown whalers stayed mostly in the Atlantic, working the grounds in a rough triangle east to the Azores and south along the northwest African coast and then west to the so-called Hatteras Grounds off the Carolinas. The recruitment of sailors in the Azores and the Cape Verde Islands was a regular practice of Provincetown whaling masters and these imported crew members often became a permanent part of the Cape-tip community, creating a cosmopolitan culture that was unique. The excellence of Provincetown whalemen was such that many who studied the industry made the claim that the best harpooners and steersmen came from the town.

Whalemen were paid in shares or "lays." Typically, the captain of the ship received 1/8th to 1/15th of the value of the catch. The first mate could expect 1/18th and the second mate, 1/28th.

Young crewmembers that lacked experience were lucky to get 1/175th of the ship's profit. Usually because of their status as "greenhands," neophyte sailors began a cruise already owing $125 for what they drew for necessary pre-sail expenses. After a successful two-year voyage, these whaling rookies would receive about $225, leaving a net of about $100 for two years at sea. Never content to stay at this level, many Provincetown whalemen eventually worked their way up to mate and captain where the rewards of a successful voyage could solidify a man's social and economic position for the rest of his life. The logbooks of some of these men reveal a hard-nosed practicality and an excellent sense of seamanship.

They survived unpredictable whales, hostile natives and raging storms.

When Captain E. Parker Cook attempted to throw a lance into a sperm whale in the Atlantic in 1850, he found that the whale had its own ideas. The wounded creature attacked his ship, damaging it to the point that he was barely able to bring it into Fayal in the Azores for repairs. But Captain Cook first made certain the whale was dead and before seeking safety he took more than one hundred barrels of oil from his adversary, which amounted to a considerable sum.

Captain Stephen A. Ryder, master of the bark *N.D. Chase* on several Atlantic whaling voyages, shot it out with several Arabs at Cintra Bay on a cruise in 1856. He killed one of the natives and two years later, with his wife and two sons along with him, he went ashore and purchased the skull as a souvenir to show them.

Rugged weather caused the loss of many Provincetown whalers. The whaling brig *Ardent* was off the Azores in 1823 when she ran into a September hurricane. Captain Samuel Soper tried to rig a sea anchor and keep the bow into the wind but the storm took away the ship's masts and forced the crew to take refuge in the smashed deckhouse. The vessel righted herself but stayed awash because of the amount of sea water in the hull. For almost a month the crew suffered from cold and hunger, some expiring from exposure. The survivors were picked up by a British packet vessel and brought to shore. Only the captain and the mate returned home to Provincetown.

In another incident in 1846, the brig *Rienzi* was lost near the island of Bermuda. Of the crew of twenty-one, only five men survived the sinking after riding in an open whaleboat for four days without provisions.

Without a doubt, Provincetown's most celebrated whaling master was Captain John Atkins Cook. Beginning his career as a harpooner aboard the schooner *William Martin* in 1879, Cook experienced a forty-year career as a whaler. He rose to command his own ships and pushed out to the Pacific in the 1890s to engage in Arctic whaling.

As controversial as he was colorful, Captain Cook was one of the last of the handful of Pacific whalers who would winter over in the frozen north so as to be in position to cruise for whales in the Beaufort Sea during the ice-free months of July and August. Captain Cook returned to Provincetown in 1906 after a forty-five month Arctic voyage that saw his ship take few whales, his crew mutiny, and his wife suffer acute depression. Undeterred by all this, he had a new vessel built in Maine and he continued to sail her in the Atlantic in search of whales until 1916. Later, he was owner of the famous whaler *Charles W. Morgan*, finally severing his ties with whaling and Provincetown in the mid-1920s when he moved to Florida to become an orange grower.

Long after Nantucket saw the end of her dominance in the whaling trade, and even beyond the reign of New Bedford as the whaling capital of New England, Provincetown was still in the business. In fact, Provincetown remained in the whaling business through 1925 when the schooner *John R. Manta* returned to the Cape tip with three hundred barrels of oil as the last vessel to complete a whaling voyage in New England.

Pacific Guano Company of Penzance Point

Penzance Point in Woods Hole is one of Falmouth's most exclusive developments. Beautiful homes dot the rim of Great Harbor and the gentle sea breezes that come up from the Elizabeth Islands provide an atmosphere of comfort and serenity. In the early part of this century the area became an exclusive home away from home for New York bankers and wealthy Boston socialites. It is the sort of place that exemplifies the finest in Cape Cod living styles.

A century ago, this section of Falmouth was anything but a setting for the affluent. It was the working-class district of the town and a decidedly blue-collar zone inhabited by Irish workers who toiled in the odorous service of the thriving Pacific Guano Company. Woods Hole in that period was a place to be avoided by those with gentle nasal sensitivities.

The guano industry was, for a time in the nineteenth century, the most important employer in Falmouth. The business was started on Long Neck in 1863 and utilized the bird droppings that were shipped there for processing from islands in the Caribbean and Pacific. The need for organic fertilizer was growing both in the United States and Europe, and the Pacific Guano Company entered an expanding market in a time of great demand. With its headquarters in Boston and additional facilities in Beaufort and Charleston, South Carolina, the enterprise employed more than thirty ships to bring the odorous ingredients to Woods Hole for processing.

The actual process of converting the guano to fertilizer involved mixing decaying fish, amply supplied by local fishermen, and sulfur with the guano. The natural phosphate contained in the bird droppings combined with the nitrogen in the fish to produce an effective, if malodorous, commercial fertilizer. The company used Great Harbor as its shipping point, and on some occasions more than a dozen vessels would be loading near Ram Island. As the business grew, the need for efficient land transportation encouraged the building of the Woods Hole branch of the Old Colony Railroad in 1872. Horse-drawn wagons hauled tons of fertilizer to the waiting rail cars off Luscombe Avenue.

A good portion of Falmouth's Irish population can trace its

ancestry to the laborers who worked in the guano plant. So many Irish were brought in to work the industry that Falmouth's first Catholic church, St. Joseph's, was built in 1882 to take care of them. For at least part of this period, workers were housed in dormitories on Bar Neck Road and later in the old Breakwater Hotel.

The company failed suddenly in February of 1889, due in large part to mismanagement rather than because of lack of demand for its product. It appears that someone on the management side was playing fast and loose with receipts while "cooking the books" for the auditors. When a Lynn, Massachusetts bank called in its loan, the company was short of cash and couldn't make the payment. In what one company official called a case of "pure cussedness," the bank sent County Sheriff Alfred Crocker into the plant to seize the assets and padlock the facility. More than one hundred workers lost their jobs in the closure. Some 40,000 tons of processed fertilizer awaited shipment to eager customers. Although this inventory was eventually sold, the company never opened again.

The factory itself was torn down in 1894. A little more than a decade later the first large estates were carved from the land on Penzance Point and today, perhaps with the exception of some extremely healthy gardens, there is nothing to even hint at what was once an important Cape Cod industry.

A nineteenth century newspaper advertisement states that Pacific Guano Company produces "the leading manufactured fertilizer no matter what our competitors say to the contrary." (J. Coogan Collection)

Chapter 4

Lost at Sea—
Cape Shipwrecks

A purple sky and a green sea converge on the horizon, a distant ship chugging north between the two, crashing forward through waves of whitecaps. It is a fishing boat, staying clear of the shoals, passing along her route the graves of more than a thousand vessels that wrecked here over the centuries. Their bones remain buried beneath the waters and the sands, occasionally awakening from their long sleep at the whim of the tides washing away their tombs.

Tales centuries old wash in with the Atlantic waves crashing along the outer arm of the Cape. These outer shores and her treacherous shoals and bars are like a spider's web in waiting ... waiting for unsuspecting ships to become gnarled in their watery threads from Provincetown to Monomoy. Each grave, whether resting beneath wave or beneath sand, is a hallowed place where man and nature did battle, and nature triumphed.

"Sacred to the memory of 57 citizens of Truro who were lost in seven vessels, which foundered at sea in the memorable gale of Oct 3, 1841" reads this monument at the Congregational Church cemetery atop Truro's Hill of Churches. (J. Sheedy photo)

Still visible at low tide are the iron remains of the bark Frances that wrecked at Head of the Meadow beach in Truro in December 1872. (J. Sheedy photo)

Sparrowhawk – The Cape's First Wreck

In December 1626, six years after the Pilgrims arrived at Cape Cod on board the *Mayflower*, a 36-ton, two-masted ketch-rigged ship approached the peninsula. She was only one-fifth the size of the 180-ton *Mayflower*.

The vessel, named *Sparrowhawk*, was en route to Virginia from England. She was forty feet in length with a twenty-eight foot keel. She carried twenty-five passengers and crew, all tired from their six-week journey. They were running low on food and were already out of water (and beer! according to Pilgrim William Bradford's journal). The master, ill with scurvy, gave orders from his cot.

They found themselves well north of their Virginia destination just as the passengers and crew of the *Mayflower* found themselves six years earlier. Just like the *Mayflower*, the *Sparrowhawk* sailed as far south as Chatham, picking her way along the shoals. Unlike the *Mayflower's* captain, though, who turned his vessel away from these dangerous waters, the *Sparrowhawk's* master ventured closer to shore near Monomoit in an effort to search for food and water. Eventually the ship grounded on a bar.

Meanwhile, Monomoyick Indians who were watching the vessel moving along the coast gathered on the beach to greet the stranded travelers. The *Sparrowhawk* crew must have been surprised and relieved to find that these "savages" not only spoke English but were also friendly with William Bradford and his band at Plymouth. The Indians offered to carry a message to Bradford, which they did along with two members from the *Sparrowhawk* crew, walking the entire length of the Cape up to Plymouth.

Bradford responded immediately. He and a small group from Plymouth sailed across Cape Cod Bay, landing at Namskaket Creek to journey by land the rest of the way. With him he brought materials to repair the damaged vessel. Bradford stayed long enough to help with repairs and buy corn from the Indians. He left for Plymouth believing the *Sparrowhawk* and her crew would be on their way to Virginia.

Shortly after his return, Bradford was notified that the

Sparrowhawk wrecked again off Nauset in a storm, this time seemingly for good. The crew asked if they could spend the winter at Plymouth. Bradford agreed, and so, with the help of Indian guides, the passengers and crew of the *Sparrowhawk* made the long trek to the Plantation. After a nine month stay at Plymouth the crew of the *Sparrowhawk* departed on two barks bound for Virginia. In Nauset, the natives burned the wrecked *Sparrowhawk* down to her waterline. What remained of her was buried in the sands, emerging briefly during the latter part of the eighteenth century to earn that stretch of sand the name Old Ship Beach. In 1863 she was uncovered again and for two years curious treasure seekers picked at her remains. Her oak timbers and English elm keel, embalmed in the sand and marsh of the forever changing coastline for two and a half centuries, were found to be well preserved. Determined to be the *Sparrowhawk*, and considered the Cape's very first shipwreck, her bones were exhumed to tour New England. For a time they were displayed at Boston Common, finally landing at Pilgrim Hall on Court Street in Plymouth in 1889 where they remain to this day.

Sparrowhawk exists as the only known remains of a seventeenth century transatlantic vessel. To see her frail skeleton of natural lumber ribs is to truly appreciate the courage of those from centuries ago who risked all in order to find freedom in a New World.

When Ships Collide

Some vessels just could not seem to navigate the Cape waters without bumping into other ships. Such was the case with the *H. F. Dimock*, which was involved in two notable accidents, both taking place in Pollock Rip Slue off the coast of Chatham. On the morning of July 23, 1892 she happened upon her first victim, the 285-foot, three-masted schooner yacht *Alva* owned by millionaire William K. Vanderbilt.

The fog that morning was thick and the *Alva*, which was traveling to Newport, Rhode Island, anchored to wait for it to lift. Out of the bank came the *Dimock*, bound from New York to Boston, colliding with the yacht. The *Alva* sank swiftly yet all on board were safely transferred to the *Dimock*. Four days later, the wreck of the *Alva* figured in another accident. The *Everett Webster*, a 140-foot, two-masted schooner, ran into the sunken wreckage of the *Alva*. The yacht was later blown up as it was a navigational menace.

Seventeen years later, the *Dimock* was involved in another accident in the very same waters. Again she was traveling in foggy conditions. The date was March 10, 1909; the other vessel was the *Horatio Hall*. As the *Hall* began to sink after the collision, her passengers and crew were transferred to the damaged *Dimock*. The *Dimock* herself was settling by the bow so once the *Hall's* passengers and crew were rescued the captain of the *Dimock* ordered his vessel intentionally grounded at Nauset Beach to prevent her from sinking.

Some five years later, the *H. F. Dimock* was one of the larger vessels to participate in the parade of ships to herald the opening of the Cape Cod Canal in 1914. Somehow she managed to make her way through the entire winding length of the canal without colliding with another vessel!

• • •

A thick fog lingered over the waters off Nantucket and enveloped the shipping traffic on the morning of January 23, 1909. Within the fog traveled the two principal players of the high seas drama about to unfold: the Italian liner *Florida* carrying about one thousand passengers and crew, and the 15,000-ton White Star Liner *Republic* carrying about seven hundred people. White Star was the British line that would, three years later, launch the *Titanic* and her sister ship, the *Olympic*.

Of course, in those days ships were without radar and by the time the two vessels were within visual range it was too late to avoid collision. The *Florida* sliced into the *Republic*, delivering a fatal wound. As the *Republic* began to sink her passengers were transferred to the *Florida*, though her own seaworthiness was in question. Yet she was the only ship on the scene.

On board the *Republic*, radio operator Jack Binns remained at his wireless station sending out distress calls. One of the ships to receive the news was the *RMS Baltic*, which three years later would race to the scene of the *Titanic* disaster after receiving her distress call over the wireless.

The *Baltic* arrived at the scene of the collision, but in the fog had difficulty finding the two vessels. All afternoon the search was conducted. Finally, the vessels were located that evening and the survivors were then transferred from the two crippled liners to the *Baltic*. The *Republic* sank on the following day while under tow. In all, only six people were lost in the disaster, all believed killed by the initial collision.

Radio operator Binns' valiant efforts would be credited with saving some 1,700 lives that day. He would be hailed as a hero on both sides of the Atlantic. And the value of Marconi's wireless radio as a ship-to-shore or even ship-to-ship communicator, especially in times of disaster when lives could be saved, was for the first time realized on a grand scale.

Longfellow

Some ships call to us from the grave. Others SCREAM!

Back on September 9, 1904, the 413-ton steamer *Longfellow*, at one time an excursion vessel built back in the 1870s and named to honor the famous poet, was hauling a dangerous cargo up the backside of the Cape. In her holds were some three hundred tons of dynamite en route to Portsmouth, New Hampshire when she ran into a nor'easter off Orleans and began to take on water.

By the time she reached Highland Light she was rolling in the heavy seas and the crew feared her shifting cargo might explode. They scrambled into two lifeboats and rowed away from the powder keg toward the glow of Coston flares held by surfmen on the beach. Crews from Pamet River and High Head lifesaving stations stood ready with those from Highland station should a rescue be necessary. Sixteen crewmen from the *Longfellow* were brought ashore without casualties.

Life on these outer Cape shores returned to normal by the next morning and the *Longfellow*, which subsequently sank, was forgotten like a stone skipped across the waters of a pond after the ripples die away ... until the night of November 13. On that evening a gale swept the seas into a boil and the activity must have awakened the *Longfellow* from her two-month sleep, slamming her sunken hull and her temperamental cargo against the ocean floor.

Two large explosions were felt that night across the Lower Cape within a fifteen-minute period. The cause of the ruckus was discovered over the days to follow as large numbers of dead fish washed up along the beaches with mangled wreckage from the steamer *Longfellow*, which sank two months earlier.

The Chilling Tale of the Castagna

The details concerning the wreck of the *Castagna* can make you shiver. En route from Montevideo, Uruguay to Weymouth, Massachusetts in February 1914 with a cargo of guano, the *Castagna* was an 843-ton Italian iron bark with a compliment of thirteen sparsely clad crewmen. Having begun their journey in warmer climes south of the equator, Captain Guiseppe Gevi and his crew never considered the colder temperatures of winter in the northern hemisphere. By the time the vessel arrived in northeast waters the crewmen were painfully underdressed for the occasion and probably wishing they were back at Uruguay.

Unaccustomed to sailing under such winter conditions where lines and rigging can become blocks of ice, the ship and crew were easy prey for the bars off Wellfleet. Over the course of the day leading up to the wreck they wandered aimlessly up and down the coast, either lost or confused or both. The ship's anchors were frozen up and therefore could not be lowered to save her from doom. She was a shipwreck waiting to happen.

Lifesavers at Cahoon Hollow Station watched the vessel throughout the day and were not at all surprised to find that by 5 a.m. the next morning, February 17, she finally ran aground about three and a half miles south of the station.

The barefooted crew of the *Castagna* climbed up into the frigid rigging to avoid being swept away by the sea crashing over the decks below. Two deckhouses were washed away as were two men who slipped from the rigging. One of those men was Captain Gevi. The remaining men were growing weak by the time the crews of the Cahoon Hollow and Nauset lifesaving stations fired their first shot from the Lyle gun into the rigging of the wrecked vessel. Two

more lines were fired yet the men of the Italian ship were too
weakened by the cold to climb after them. Finally, one line was
retrieved and tied off to the mast of the *Castagna*, but it was tied
too low to employ the breeches buoy. The lifesavers realized that a
surfboat would need to be launched if anyone was to be saved.

Of the thirteen *Castagna* crewmen, eight survived the ordeal.
Since the wreck occurred near the Marconi Wireless Station, the
survivors were brought there to be warmed back to life and fed.
Later, they were transported to Carney Hospital in Boston as many
of the men suffered frostbite. A couple of men required the ampu-
tation of some of their fingers and toes.

Meanwhile, the dead crewmen in the rigging were removed in
the days that followed and buried in the local cemetery, but the
body of Captain Gevi, who fell into the sea, was not to be found.

About one year later, the wreck of the *Castagna* had its gruesome
conclusion when a body was discovered on the beach protruding
from the sand. It turned out to be Captain Gevi, and remarkably
his body survived a year in the waters off Wellfleet without
decomposing. The only answer to this mystery is that it froze in
those February seas of 1914 and then was buried beneath the
shifting sands to become naturally preserved!

Seth Weeks - Survivor of the Essex

Although Barnstable was not a major whaling port like
Provincetown, Nantucket or New Bedford, she was home port to a
number of whaling vessels during the eighteenth and nineteenth
centuries. One such vessel, the brig *March*, was very nearly the last
Barnstable whaler when Captain Seth Weeks of West Barnstable
took her out to the Atlantic whaling grounds on June 4, 1846. She
returned a little more than one year later in August 1847 with 250
barrels of sperm whale oil.

Her master was born March 4, 1803 in Plymouth to Captain
Zenas Weeks (born November 19, 1775 in Barnstable) and Chloe
Blossom (born August 15, 1773 in Sandwich). Though Captain Seth
Weeks would spend sixty years at sea on a number of vessels, he
would forever be known as one of only eight survivors of the most

Located in West Barnstable is the headstone of Captain Seth Weeks, the last survivor of the Essex disaster. (J. Sheedy photo)

horrific whaling disasters of all time. It involves a tale so incredible that Herman Melville fashioned his stoving of Ahab's ship *Pequod* by the white whale Moby Dick after this factual event. As it turns out, the factual account is more terrible than fiction.

Perhaps nothing can compare to the terrible events that surround what is known as the *Essex* Disaster. In a time when Nantucket was the whaling capital of the world, the *Essex* was one of the port's more successful vessels. Built in 1796, her four previous voyages, beginning in 1804, resulted in many thousands of tons of sperm whale oil harvested. Stepping in as master of the *Essex* for her fifth voyage was Captain George Pollard Jr. He previously served as First Mate. Also aboard was junior crewman Seth Weeks, then only sixteen years old. Years later he would go on to become a whaling captain in his own right, but he would first have to survive the *Essex*.

The *Essex* left Nantucket on August 12, 1819, rounded Cape

Horn in January 1820, and then made for the whaling grounds of the South Pacific. After one year at sea she filled one thousand barrels with oil. It was business as usual, until that fateful November day that would inspire Melville's novel.

On November 20, 1820, while many of the men were out in the whaleboats, an 85-foot sperm whale attacked the *Essex*. Twice the whale rammed the vessel and left her to founder.

Stranded without a ship, the captain and his nineteen crewmen set off in three whaleboats on the incredible two thousand-mile journey to South America to the east. Closer were the Marquesas Islands, but the captain balked at the idea for it was believed that cannibals inhabited those islands. As it would turn out, his decision would hold an ironic twist of fate.

Battling rough, shark infested seas in leaking boats, the men saw their food rations (six hundred pounds of bread and sixty-five gallons of water taken from the sinking *Essex*) quickly spoiling due to salt water. Fortunately, on December 20, after one month at sea in open boats, they made landfall at what they believed to be Ducie Island, an uninhabited "piece of rock" six miles long by three miles wide in the middle of the Pacific Ocean. The island featured inhospitable terrain marked by steep cliffs. There the crew discovered some food in the form of birds' eggs, shellfish, pepper grass, small berries and fresh water. Though the island was much safer than the open boats, the food supply was certainly not enough to feed twenty men and their chances of rescue by a passing ship were slim at best.

So it was decided on December 27 to cast off again, this time for Easter Island, which rested somewhere to the east. Three of the crew, Weeks included, decided to stay behind rather then gamble on another journey. He probably considered himself lucky to survive one month at sea adrift under a terrible sun and with minimal food supplies, and could not imagine that his luck would continue. Joining him on the island were William Wright, also of Barnstable, and Thomas Chapple. For Weeks and his two comrades it would turn out to be a good decision indeed.

Life on the island, though depressing, was bearable and at first there seemed to be food and water enough for the three to live on.

Soon, though, the birds left the island. Then the three men had difficulty obtaining fresh water at the spring and were reduced to drinking water that collected in rocks after the rains. At times they would go for six days without water. Attempts to dig a well were in vain. To stay alive they were forced to suck the blood of small birds they managed to catch.

Meanwhile, they virtually killed off the crab population and found great difficulty in catching fish since they had no fishing tackle. Their only chance of survival now rested in the success of those in the boats making their way for Easter Island.

A discovery of eight skeletons in a cave on the island representing the crew members of the wrecked ship *Elizabeth* could not have bolstered Week's faltering hopes of rescue. But rescue did eventually come, in the form of the English vessel *Surrey* on April 8, 1821 after one hundred and two days. It is said that the *Surrey* arrived at Ducie Island and her crew found nobody there. Before leaving the area, the captain decided to check nearby Henderson Island and there they found Weeks, Wright and Chapple. Apparently Captain Pollard, who upon his rescue asked that the Pacific-bound *Surrey* make a detour to pick up his three remaining crewmen, miscalculated their position and thus misjudged the identity of the small rocky island.

As for those poor souls who ventured out from the island in the whaleboats for Easter Island, here is their terrible story:

Captain Pollard, First Mate Owen Chase and Second Mate Matthew Joy commanded the three boats. On January 11, 1821 Joy died and Third Mate Obed Hendricks took command of the boat. The very next day Chase's boat was separated from the boats of Pollard and Hendricks in a fierce storm.

Now two months at sea and food having long since been consumed, starvation threatened the lives of those remaining. Winds carried them well south and east of Easter Island, forcing the men to make for South America - a seemingly impossible feat. Some began to go crazy, others found their speech and eyesight affected. Then came the deaths of Charles Shorter in Hendricks' boat and Isaac Cole in Chase's boat. With the extremity of the situation, these latest deaths provided the remaining crew members with their only means of survival. No longer were the dead crew members to be buried at sea, but instead, eaten.

On January 28, Hendricks' boat was separated from Pollard's in rough seas and was never seen again. By the time Chase's boat was rescued by the brig *Indian* on February 18 only three very thin and bearded crewmen remained. Captain Pollard's boat would not be picked up until February 23, after three months adrift, by the Nantucket whaler *Dauphin*, but before then the course of events in that whaleboat would go from terrible to nightmarish.

On February 1, Pollard and the three remaining crew members, having already devoured the others who were on board, decided to draw lots to determine who would be sacrificed so that the others might survive. Once the victim was chosen, lots were again drawn to decide who would be the one to pull the trigger. How can anyone fathom the extremities that drove these men to such actions?!

Fortunately for the young Seth Weeks, he was spared the horrors that took place aboard the three whaleboats during the second leg of the journey. The vessel *Surrey* carried him to Port Jackson, Australia. There he signed on as a member of the *Surrey* crew for the voyage to England, arriving there on July 3, 1822. It would not be until late-1822 when Weeks would return home to Barnstable, three years after the *Essex* left Nantucket.

Weeks sailed on many other whaling voyages out of New Bedford after his return. He would go on to become a master himself, of the whaler *George Howland* out of New Bedford from 1838 to 1841, and the *March* out of Barnstable from 1846 to 1847, and later out of Yarmouth from 1849 to 1850.

He and his wife Content A. Jenkins (1816-1893) had no children. In 1879, at the age of 75, Weeks retired from the sea. While in his old age, he lost his sight, and on September 12, 1887 suffered an apoplectic shock at the breakfast table of his Osterville home. He died later that evening at the age of 84 years. In the September 20, 1887 issue of *The Barnstable Patriot* his death notice appears, naming him as the last of the *Essex* survivors. He is buried at West Barnstable.

As for two of Weeks' fellow shipmates, Captain Pollard wrecked the very next ship he commanded and never sailed again. He spent the later years of his life as a night watchman on the Nantucket docks. First Mate Chase went on to become a master of whaling vessels and led a successful seafaring existence. In his final years, though, he was apparently plagued by the fear of starvation. He would purchase more food than he needed and was often found hiding the food in unlikely places around his house ... just in case.

The Great "Portland Gale"

In November 1898, the people of Cape Cod were preparing for the advent of the twentieth century. The nineteenth century they were leaving behind was one of unparalleled successes. Cape Cod clipper ships and their captains ruled the world's oceans. Provincetown, Nantucket and Edgartown whaling ships brought riches in whale oil back from the Pacific.

A factory in Sandwich made that town one of the world's greatest producers of glassware. Falmouth became the country's largest grower of strawberries. A cranberry industry was born in the bogs of Dennis, Harwich and West Barnstable. And hundreds of saltworks along the shorelines harvested valuable salt from the sea. In the nineteenth century, Cape Cod matured from her colonial upbringing to play a major role in our country's history.

Yet, the latter years of the century brought with it decline. Clipper ships were passé, replaced by steam engines. Whale oil was no longer in demand, neither was salt from the sea as salt mines were discovered out west. The glassworks of Sandwich crumbled and bad times followed. A depression settled over the Cape, not helped by the nationwide depression of 1893. By 1898, the country rallied around the battle cry "Remember the *Maine!*" and a war erupted with Spain. The people of Cape Cod looked to the next century with a degree of cautious optimism. But first, they would have to face the "*Portland* Gale."

November 26, 1898 began peaceful enough, in no way suggesting the doom that was to come over the hours and days to follow. During the course of the day the seas began to grow with an increasing north wind. Around mid-afternoon, New York was reporting heavy snows and heavy winds. By nightfall, prudent sea captains were heading their vessels for a safe harbor. Meanwhile, at Boston's India Wharf, some 175 Thanksgiving passengers boarded the steamer *Portland* for an overnight one hundred-mile sojourn home after the holiday. By morning, they imagined, they would be docking at the vessel's namesake Maine city. At 7 p.m. the *Portland* left India Wharf. Little did she know of the fate that awaited her.

Along a narrow peninsula boasting more than a thousand shipwrecks over the past three and three quarter centuries, the *Portland* is perhaps the greatest of all Cape Cod shipwrecks.

Built in 1890 by the New England Shipbuilding Company of Bath, Maine, the *Portland* was a 291-foot long, 2,280-ton paddle wheel steamer. Along with her sister ship *Bay State*, they made the daily run between Boston and Portland. The *Bay State*, incidentally, was lost off Cape Elizabeth, Maine on September 24, 1916.

The *Portland* had a maximum speed of fifteen knots. Her master in 1898 was fifty-five-year-old Captain Hollis Henry Blanchard who was known as being very cautious. To this day it is unclear why such a cautious man would take the *Portland* out on such an evening that would grow to become a "hundred-year-storm."

Even as she left Boston Harbor the seas were mounting and the winds were becoming fierce. Ships of all kinds passed the beautiful paddle wheel steamer as they headed in toward a safe harbor from the increasing nor'easter. Still it is impossible to understand why Captain Blanchard did not turn his vessel around and head back to India Wharf.

The storm that would become known as the "*Portland* Gale" is believed to be the combination of two storms that collided over southeastern New England. One storm was coming from the south. The captain and owners of the *Portland* were well aware of this storm and, it is assumed, reasoned that their vessel could outrun it on her way north to her homeport. This thinking is confirmed by the fact that the *Bay State*, scheduled to make the trip south from Portland to Boston that evening, remained safely at her Portland, Maine berth rather than heading south into the storm.

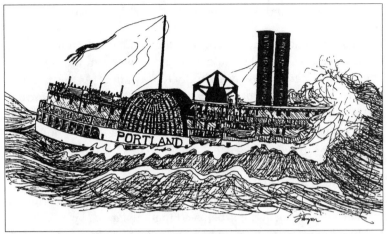

The last moments of the steamer Portland, lost in the great gale of November 1898. (by J. Thompson)

The Portland Steam Packet Company, though, was not aware of a second storm carrying hurricane force winds racing southeast from the Great Lakes.

Twenty minutes before eight that evening snow began to fall. By 9 p.m. the *Portland* was sighted off Gloucester, about three miles off shore. Another vessel witnessed her battling large waves near Thatcher Island, off Gloucester. Again, the ships that sighted her at this hour were heading for port.

Perhaps the master of the *Portland* was having second thoughts, but with the growing storm Captain Blanchard knew he would risk capsizing the ship by turning a port or starboard side to such large seas. History tells that he should have taken the risk, yet Blanchard's policy was to keep the vessel's bow pointed into the onslaught and to hang on for dear life until the storm subsided.

Between 9:30 and 11 p.m., it is believed, the two storms converged to become one. The snows became very heavy; the winds shifted from north to northeast, reaching about 40 miles per hour at 11 p.m. and growing steadily throughout the night until reaching 70 miles per hour around 3 a.m. At Nantucket, 90-mile-per-hour winds were measured. A tempest was unleashed, pounding the Cape and her waters with a force that surpassed even the great

October Gale of 1841. Cape Codders never saw a storm of such magnitude.

According to eyewitness accounts, the *Portland* was still off Gloucester at 11 p.m. She could make no forward progress, but continued to battle the waves simply to stay afloat. At this point Blanchard was, no doubt, merely attempting to outlast the storm.

At midnight it is believed that the *Portland* was off Eastern Point Light near Norman's Woe, possibly attempting to reach Gloucester Harbor. By now she had been at sea for five hours and traveled only thirty miles.

The wind reached 60 miles per hour or more at that hour and still the storm had yet to reach its height. That would not occur until around 5 a.m. and it is believed that the *Portland* was still fighting her way upon the rough seas. In fact, she may have survived to 7 a.m., and possibly as late as 9:30 a.m. according to some reports of hearing the horn of a large steamer off Race Point that morning.

Between the hours of midnight and daybreak of November 27 the *Portland* was pushed by the storm across Massachusetts Bay to just north of Provincetown, her master Captain Blanchard, no doubt, fighting the tempest every step of the way. Imagine the terror of those hours on board the *Portland* as waves and wind slammed the ship across the fifty miles from Gloucester to Provincetown!

At daybreak a foot of snow was on the ground and the storm continued unabated. The railroad lines were hopelessly blocked and in other areas swept away completely. Telegraph lines were down and Cape Cod found herself cut off from the rest of the world. And out there, on the raging seas, hundreds of vessels and thousands of sailors battled for their lives throughout the long night and the relentless stormy days to follow.

Early the following morning, Monday, November 28, wreckage from the *Portland*, along with the wreckage from other vessels, began washing up along the beaches from Provincetown to Chatham. The *Portland*, her passengers and crew were lost somewhere northeast of Highland Light in Truro although no one knew the exact location of the wreck.

By Tuesday morning the storm had blown itself out. Nearly two hundred vessels were lost. With them drowned some five hundred people, including those who went down on the *Portland.*

With the telegraph lines down, the country learned of the disaster via France. News was cabled across the Atlantic where it was relayed back to New York via Ireland and Newfoundland. The full weight of the tragedy began to settle in with each piece of twisted wreckage and with each bloated body found along the Lower Cape coastline. The list of vessels lost or presumed lost seemed without end: *Lester A. Lewis, King Philip, F.A. Walker, Albert A. Butler, Addie E. Snow, Jordan L. Mott, James B. Pace* ... and, of course, the *Portland.*

Meanwhile, on land the damage was without precedent. Ice-laden trees were uprooted all over the Cape, numerous homes and buildings were damaged, streets were flooded. Normal life ground to a halt as Cape Codders dug out and then began to piece their homes and businesses back together.

The storm would be named for its biggest prize. Cape Codders would talk of the "*Portland* Gale" for decades to come, comparing every storm that followed to the "hundred year storm" of 1898. Even today, a century later, her memory and the memories of those souls lost to her fury command our respect.

A half century later a diver claimed to have explored the wreck in 144 feet of water about seven miles off Truro, yet the *Portland's* eventual discovery in a different spot further northwest suggests that perhaps the diver was confused over the identity of the wreck he discovered.

The *Portland* was discovered exactly ninety years after she went down just north of Race Point in an area where fishermen snagged their nets for the past century. The vessel is in a demolished state in three hundred and fifty feet of water.

Much of the *Portland* washed up with the waves in the form of wreckage. This wreckage found its way into Cape Cod homes and eventually into museums. A deck post can be viewed at the Jericho House museum in South Dennis, while at the Centerville Historical Society Museum is the *Portland's* wheel.

Today, whale watching vessels off Provincetown sail over the area where the *Portland* now rests at peace upon the sandy bottom. But when the winds grow into a gale and the waves crash with a boom upon the outer arm of the Cape, images of a paddle wheel steamer fighting the turbulent seas come to mind, forever earning the *Portland* a place in Cape Cod lore.

The S-4 Disaster

Examine the long list of Cape shipwrecks and you will come across some that are tragic, some that are sad, some that could easily have been avoided, and some that are horrific in nature. The story of the S-4 submarine is all of the above, with perhaps a singular emphasis on the horrific.

December 17, 1927 was a Saturday and the people of Provincetown went about their business as usual. A proud fishing fleet cast and hauled their nets against a sea foretelling of an approaching storm. Meanwhile, off Provincetown, the crew of the Navy submarine S-4 out of Portsmouth, New Hampshire was testing their vessel after work performed on the sub at the Charlestown Navy Yard. The morning's exercises consisted of a series of dives in the more than one hundred-foot waters and all appeared to be working in fine order. Across the water, at Wood End Coast Guard Station, Boatswain Emanuel Gracie watched the goings on with interest as he went about his duties.

Morning became afternoon and across Cape Cod Bay from Boston steamed the Coast Guard Cutter *Paulding*. The four-stack *Paulding* was a former World War I Navy destroyer that was now patrolling more domestic waters in search of rumrunners. Her travels brought her to the tip of the Cape and at precisely 3:37 p.m. she was making her way past Wood End Coast Guard Station at sixteen miles per hour, heading toward Provincetown Harbor. Neither her crew nor her master, Captain John S. Baylis, knew that below them was the S-4 submarine.

The crew of the S-4 were equally unaware of the cutter's presence. Only Boatswain Gracie at the Wood End Station was aware of the tragedy unfolding before his very eyes. In fact, he even commented just moments before to a fellow crewman at the station that he feared there might be a collision.

Though the *S-4's* periscope was above the surface, no one on the *Paulding* saw it. The submarine broke the surface just in time to receive a deathblow from the *Paulding's* bow, which sliced a hole in her hull just forward of the conning tower. The captain of the *Paulding* knew instantly what happened as it was known that these waters were used as a testing ground for Navy submarines. He immediately sent a distress message that the cutter collided with an unknown submarine off Wood End Light.

Meanwhile, beneath the surface, the crew of the *S-4* had no chance of escape. The submarine sank in five minutes to rest some 110 feet below on the floor of Cape Cod Bay. The *Paulding* lowered her boats to pick up survivors from the submarine but none were to be found. The cutter, damaged and her crew detecting no survivors from the mortally wounded sub, limped into Provincetown Harbor.

Just prior to the collision, Boatswain Gracie readied a boat just in case it was necessary. As the *Paulding* made for the harbor, Gracie rowed out to the area of water where the collision occurred and lowered his grapnel line in hopes of snagging the sub. There probably were no survivors, but he knew that any Navy rescue operations would certainly move along more swiftly if the sub was already located.

For some six hours in the most unpleasant winter conditions, much of it in darkness upon a steadily growing sea, Gracie dragged the waters in search of the wrecked submarine. Finally, at nearly 10 p.m. he found her only to have gale force winds snap his line. Exhausted and cold, he abandoned the search until morning.

Remarkably, when Gracie awoke the next morning he found that rescue operations were still not underway although the *Falcon*, a salvage vessel, had arrived at Provincetown Harbor. The *S-4's* mother ship, *Bushnell*, was on her way from Portsmouth. Wooden pontoons were being towed from New York and divers were being brought in from Newport, Rhode Island. Help was on the way, but three questions remained: Was anyone still alive on the sub? Would the help arrive on time? And even if help did arrive, was there really any way to save men trapped on a sub more than one hundred feet below the surface?

News of the collision was broadcast around America and around the world. The Secretary of the Navy, the Chief of Navy Operations and a number of admirals were all on their way to Provincetown to investigate the incident and to oversee rescue operations if such operations were necessary.

Gracie went back out in his boat and was successful in once again locating the submarine with his grapnel line. Finally the *Falcon* came alongside and, with Gracie's line, was now connected to the *S-4* below. Unfortunately, high seas made it impossible to dive to the wreck that morning so the crew of the *Falcon* and the divers who arrived from Newport waited for the gales to let up. By afternoon they could wait no longer. Somebody had to risk a dive to see if anyone was alive below.

That man would be Tom Eadie. He was aided into his diving suit and then over the side he went to follow the grapnel line to the submarine below. At the depth of more than one hundred feet, and with the wind and waves churning everything up, visibility was but a few feet. He took a hammer with him and as his feet made contact with the hull he immediately heard tapping from inside. There were men, alive, trapped in the submarine!

He tapped international Morse code on the hull with his hammer to discover that six crewmen survived the collision in the forward torpedo room. At this point it was about twenty-four hours since the collision.

Eadie then made his way along the rest of the submarine, tapping with his hammer as he went. No response did he receive. Apparently all the rest of the crew, thirty-four men in total, were dead. One can only assume that they died during those first few desperate minutes as the sub filled with water and sank to the bottom.

Returning to the surface, it was now Bill Carr's turn to dive to the *S-4* and attach an air hose. The decision made at that point by those overseeing the rescue efforts in terms of where to attach this air hose would prove to be *the* decision to ultimately determine the fates of those trapped below. At this stage of the operation they had to decide whether to attach the hose to bring fresh air to the men in the torpedo room or else to fill one of the ballast tanks in an effort to bring the sub to the surface. With rough seas growing around them they chose the latter.

So down went Carr to attach the hose to the ballast tank connection. The valves were turned and air rushed through the hose to the damaged vessel below. Yet the damage proved to be more severe than the rescuers first guessed as air bubbles began to appear on the surface foretelling of a leak in the ballast tank. As history would show, they made the wrong choice.

Weather conditions deteriorated. It was decided that one last dive would be attempted. This third dive would bring a hose below to pump fresh air into the torpedo room and thus keep the men alive until a workable rescue effort could be employed with the use of the pontoons coming by slow tugs from New York.

Fred Michaels donned his gear aboard the rolling *Falcon*, knowing that a dive in such seas was not safe, but six lives down below rested on his taking the risk. Down he went with the air hose to land atop the sub. The rocking of the ship above caused his lifeline to yank him this way and that. He slipped off the top of the sub to become embedded in the mud of the ocean floor.

Somehow, with the help of the men on the rescue vessel above who carefully pulled on his lifeline, Michaels was able to pull himself free of the mud only to find himself hopelessly entangled in the sharp wreckage of the *S-4*. He called above to the rescue ship to alert them to his situation. Another diver would need to go below to help release Michaels, so Eadie prepared for his second dive.

On the bottom, Eadie tried to untangle Michaels' lifeline but in the rough seas the task was impossible. Michaels was beginning to weaken. Eadie called above for a hacksaw, which was lowered to him. In the absolute worst of conditions he was able to cut Michaels loose so he could return to the surface. Eadie's thoughts of attaching the air hose to the submarine were quickly dashed when he tore his diving suit on a piece of the sharp wreckage that moments earlier threatened to take Michaels' life. Eadie's suit quickly began to fill with water and he had to be taken away to the surface.

Next morning, Monday, the gale grew and rescue operations were put on hold until a break in the weather. During this lull the

Falcon left the scene for Boston to transport diver Michaels to the hospital. The rescue vessel returned to the waters off Provincetown later that afternoon but still the foul weather had not abated.

Through the use of an oscillator attached to the hull of the S-4, those above could communicate via Morse code with the six men trapped on the ocean floor. The submarine crewmen asked when rescue might come. In return, messages from their families were relayed down to them. By Monday evening the air supply in the sub would be exhausted and yet the weather conditions had still not improved enough to risk a diver.

The wait continued. As the men below weakened with each poisonous breath they realized their fate. Rescue would not arrive in time. The well wishes they were receiving from their families in dots and dashes were actually farewell wishes.

Still, the plan was to attach an air hose to the sub and to send food through the torpedo tube as soon as a diver could be lowered. But it was not to be. A final message was received from the sub around 6 a.m. on Tuesday morning, roughly sixty-two hours after the collision. It said, simply, "We understand."

Finally, on Wednesday morning the storm let up and preparations were made to attempt a dive only to discover that the buoy line to the sub disconnected!

Upon hearing this news, the entire fishing fleet of Provincetown offered to sweep across the area with their draggers in order to locate the sub quickly so rescue operations could continue. Yet, the Navy declined the fishermen's offer and the *Falcon* was left alone to grope blindly with a single drag line looking for the S-4. It took them the better part of the day and wasted many valuable hours.

A diver was finally lowered, the hose was attached and fresh air was pumped into the torpedo room. Rescuers called down and waited for an answer, but no response was heard. All were dead. The rescue operation would now become a salvage operation.

Although the Navy expressed that they were in no particular hurry to salvage the sub, a Provincetown community enraged by the Navy's mishandling of the rescue operations demanded that the bodies be brought up immediately. As soon as the weather improved the divers went down to bring up the dead one by one.

The three pontoons finally arrived and on March 17, 1928, three months after the disaster, the S-4 was raised to the surface. She was towed to the Charlestown Navy Yard for repairs and was later used as an experimental vessel in the salvage of wrecked submarines and the rescue of their crews.

The public questioned the rescue operations, and wondered if everything possible was done to save the six trapped crewmen. An inquiry into the disaster initially placed blame on three individuals: the captain of the *Paulding* , the captain of the S-4 and the rear admiral in charge of the rescue operations. Later, the Secretary of the Navy pardoned the captain of the *Paulding* and the rear admiral, concentrating all blame on the dead captain of the sunken submarine.

Today, all these years later, the waters off Wood End remain haunted by the events of those cold December days. Cape Cod history will long remember the tale of six men sealed in a sarcophagus of steel on the ocean floor and of the divers who on that December afternoon tried to free them.

Wreck of the Pendleton: A Mission Impossible

On the night of February 18, 1952 a storm visited Cape Cod, churning the waters off Chatham into a boiling sea of sixty-foot waves. Upon that night, not one but two large tankers split in half in those waters thus setting the stage for one of the Cape's most courageous rescue efforts since the Monomoy Disaster of March 1902, some fifty years earlier.

The evening began with a distress call from the tanker *Fort Mercer*. She broke up in very rough seas southwest of Chatham. Coast Guard cutters from a number of stations along the northeast coast headed for the waters off Chatham while a PBY out of Salem Air Station flew over the turbulent waters searching for the stricken vessel. Although the crew of the plane had a difficult time locating the tanker in the raging storm, they eventually found her and circled over the scene to mark her location for the racing cutters.

Rescuers found that of the *Fort Mercer's* crew, some were on the stern section while others remained on the severed bow. Coast Guard cutters *Acushnet, Yakatat* and *Eastwind* swept in to pick up the *Mercer's* survivors. Thirteen of the tanker's crewmen were lost in the disaster.

Another high seas drama was taking place fifty miles away off Monomoy where a second tanker, the *Pendleton*, was drifting in two pieces. The vessel, en route to Boston, broke up at 5:30 a.m. off Provincetown, the damage to the ship knocking out the radio transmitter thus preventing the crew from sending a distress call. As the two pieces of the *Pendleton* drifted south, the crew learned of the *Fort Mercer* rescue efforts over their radio receiver, which was still operating, and they perhaps were wondering "What about us?!"

Although all rescue vessels and personnel concentrated their efforts on the *Fort Mercer*, unaware that another tanker was in the same predicament, the men at the Coast Guard station at Chatham were monitoring the two meandering radar blips of the *Pendleton*. They surmised that the two blips belonged to a large ship that broke in half as the *Fort Mercer* did. The Coast Guardsmen of Chatham had little choice, a rescue had to be attempted and they were the only crew available to make it.

Ordered to command the rescue boat was Coxswain Bernie Webber, then twenty-three years old. Webber spent that afternoon assisting fishermen in Chatham Harbor who were battening down their hatches against the growing gale, not knowing then what the evening would hold in store for him.

The evening's events would consist of sixty-foot waves and seventy-mile-per-hour winds. Webber knew, as did all those at the station, that there was a very good chance he would not return. And now he had to select a crew of three men to accompany him on this certain suicide mission. Before he could make his selection, three of his comrades - Andrew Fitzgerald, Richard Livesey and Irving Maske - stepped forward to volunteer.

At the Chatham fish pier they met up with a fisherman. Webber told the fisherman to notify his wife that he was going out to try to reach the stricken tanker. In the thirty-six-foot motorized lifeboat CG 36500 the four men from Chatham station set off into seas twice

In dry dock during the summer of 1999, the gold lifesaving medal Coast Guard lifeboat CG 36500 can usually be found "on duty" at Orleans' Rock Harbor. (J. Sheedy photo)

as high as their vessel was long and against hurricane force winds. It was an impossible rescue mission into a sea that would most likely claim four more victims.

On the way out their boat was damaged by the lashing waves. The windshield was broken, the compass and some rescue equipment were lost overboard and the engine stalled a number of times. Fitzgerald would restart the engine by hitting the carburetor with a hammer.

Without a compass or radar, the vessel picked its way over the mountainous waves with the aid of those at the Chatham station who monitored the positions of the *CG 36500* and the tanker on radar and then communicated the heading. The radio, like the engine, would cut out from time to time and during one gulf of silence Webber feared they were lost and would not find the tanker. For that moment he was considering the safety of his crew and whether they could survive the wild winter night until morning. Yet somehow, throughout all that stood in their way, the crew was able to arrive safely at the stern section of the tanker *Pendleton*.

Upon the stern were all thirty-three surviving members of the tanker's crew. After the beating they took on the way out Webber actually considered abandoning his Coast Guard lifeboat for the apparent safety of the huge stern of the *Pendleton*, but he knew he had a mission to accomplish.

Next came the most difficult task of transferring the men from the *Pendleton* to the lifeboat below, a lifeboat rocking madly in the violent seas. The Jacob's ladder was employed and one by one the crewmen crawled down over the side of the listing tanker. The CG 36500 made two dozen passes, each time one or two crewmen from the *Pendleton* would drop to the passing lifeboat below. On a half dozen occasions the men missed the boat completely and fell into the ocean, yet each time they were plucked free of the waves by the Coast Guard crew.

At some point, Webber realized that his boat could only hold so many people. He considered, for only a moment, the possibility of abandoning some members of the crew on board the tanker in order to save those that he could transport back to safety. Webber then made what could have been a fatal decision. He would either rescue everybody or nobody. No one would be left behind.

Unfortunately, one crewman was lost in the transfer. George Myers, a three hundred-pound man who was called "Tiny" by his fellow crewmen, helped his comrades make their escape off the doomed tanker. He offered to be the last man off the vessel and as his turn came he fell to the sea below, lost beneath the waves.

With thirty-six men on a lifeboat with a maximum capacity of twenty-three, the Coast Guard crew ordered the men from the tanker to huddle low in the boat and to hang on for their lives. The boat motored away from the tanker's stern and headed landward for what they assumed would prove to be an arduous journey to safety.

Their navigational equipment having been washed away, the crew made their best guess as to where land might be and hoped to at least find the beaches of Monomoy Island where they could crash land their boat. The landing, they figured, would be more dangerous than the initial trip out to the tanker. Some men would most likely not make it to shore once the gigantic waves capsized the boat in the pounding surf. It was a chance they would all have to take.

As they started in, a message came over the radio from a Coast Guard cutter well off shore. Wanting to participate in the rescue efforts, the cutter told Webber to motor his vessel *out to sea* in order to intercept the cutter that could not come closer to land for fear of hitting the shoals. For a number of minutes Webber overheard Coast Guard officials arguing over the radio the pros and cons of motoring the overcrowded lifeboat out to sea to meet the cutter so that the survivors could be transferred to the larger boat. Webber's decision was made ... he chose to shut off his radio with the officials in mid-chatter and head his boat toward land as quickly as possible.

It was now more than five hours since the *CG 36500* left the fish pier at Chatham Harbor. As his vessel battled the waves on its way in Webber began to become concerned. He figured they should have reached Monomoy by now, that is, if they were heading in the right direction. Suddenly, in the gloom Webber saw a flashing red light. As the lifeboat drew nearer he recognized it as a buoy ... the buoy marking the entrance to Chatham Harbor!

Remarkably, the small boat emerged from a raging sea threatening to swallow it whole. The *CG 36500* motored right up to the fish pier where the impossible rescue operation commenced earlier that evening and where, at 11 p.m., it concluded.

The crew from the *Pendleton*, many being injured, chilled to the bone or in a state of shock, were helped out of the lifeboat by a large crowd of Chatham residents who gathered at the pier hoping and praying for the safe return of *CG 36500*. Many of the tanker crew were themselves praying and sobbing at their fortune.

Webber, watching all this from the stern of his Coast Guard vessel, felt the past hours come crashing down upon him. A force greater than himself, greater than his crew, greater than his boat or the tanker, greater even than the storm itself certainly guided them over every wave. They challenged the tempest, and they won.

Overcome by the moment, the brave and rugged Bernie Webber wiped away tears in the company of his crewmen.

The four boys from the Chatham station were later awarded the Gold Lifesaving Medal for their bravery, the Guard's highest honor. Despite the accolades and press that followed the event, Coxswain Webber did not consider his actions that evening as "heroic." He admitted he was afraid. He also admitted that his mission as a member of the Coast Guard did not afford him many options.

Days later, the cutter *Eastward* and the tug *M. Moran* towed the bow section of the *Fort Mercer* to Rhode Island. The Coast Guard would later sink the *Mercer's* stern section as it was a menace to navigation. As for the stern section of the *Pendleton*, it would remain a landmark resting on its side in the waters off Monomoy for the next quarter century. Storms in the years to follow, notably the Blizzard of 1978, tossed her about and made her a potential hazard. She was dynamited in July 1979.

As for the *CG 36500*, she was decommissioned in 1968 and, because she was a Gold Lifesaving Medal boat, was given to the Cape Cod National Seashore. For the next thirteen years she fell into disrepair until she was presented to the Orleans Historical Society in 1981 and restored. Today she proudly remains on display at Rock Harbor.

The waters off the Lower Cape are like a great book filled with stories of shipwrecks, of shipwrecked crews and of lifesavers. Earning its chapter in the book are the vessels and events and men who made a certain February night in 1952 part of the Cape Cod tale.

Chapter
5

Lighthouses, Lightships & Lifesavers

Perhaps the grandest image of Cape Cod is that of a tall and mighty lighthouse high upon a cliff overlooking the sea. At one time there were eighteen beacons shining across the Cape from Nobska Point to Race Point, cautioning vessels to beware, blinking their beams through fog and rain and winter snow.

Aiding these lighthouses were lightships offshore, marking the dangerous shoals along the coast. Life on these lightships was a combination of long stretches of boredom contrasted with episodes of extreme terror. Joining the lighthouses and lightships were thirteen lifesaving stations that lined the shoreline from Provincetown to Monomoy from 1872 to 1915. Surfmen from these legendary stations walked the beaches throughout the night, keeping an eye out for vessels in distress.

Lighthouses, lightships and lifesaving stations – each institution attempting to demystify and defeat this beast called shipwreck.

Highland, Nauset and Chatham Lights

With a face turned toward the sea one sets off to discover the peninsula's magnificent lighthouses. And perhaps the best place to begin is with a trek to the "big three" that guard the outer Cape beaches. It is difficult to consider one without examining the other two, for the three are related, or rather, their histories are related.

The three are Highland Light (also known as Cape Cod Light), Nauset Light and Chatham Light - stoic towers braving the years, the nor'easters, the hurricanes and the eroding cliffs.

Highland Light is the site of the Cape's very first lighthouse. She was built in 1797 and was the only light to meet mariners along their dark and dangerous journey from Nantucket to Boston. In 1808 her beam was joined by those of two wooden lighthouses built in the general location of the current Chatham Light. Highland had fifteen lamps burning while each of the Chatham towers had but six. The Chatham twins were movable, therefore serving as range lights designed to mark the forever-changing harbor entrance. By lining up the two lights as one approached, a mariner was able to safely navigate through the channel.

By 1837 it was decided that the gulf of darkness between Highland and Chatham needed illumination. So three small brick lighthouses were constructed on a cliff near the spot where the current Nauset Light now stands. Four years later, the two Chatham lighthouses surrendered to the eroding cliffs. Two new brick towers with nine lamps each were built, each later replaced by a 4th order Fresnel lens system.

Meanwhile, in 1857, Highland Light was deemed unsafe and was completely rebuilt. She received a 1st order Fresnel lens - the largest available at that time. During that same year the three towers of Nauset were upgraded to include 6th order Fresnel lenses, which were upgraded fifteen years later to 4th order.

The year 1879 saw the southernmost tower of the second generation Chatham twins tumble over the side of the cliff, a cliff that lost more than two hundred feet in less than a ten-year period! Chatham operated with only one tower for the next two years until the cliff finally took the north tower. Two new iron shelled light-

Highland Lighthouse, built in 1857, in her new location after being moved back from the eroding cliffs. (J. Sheedy photo)

houses were built further back from the cliff; the south tower remaining today as Chatham Light.

One has to realize when considering the past generations of lighthouses lining the coast from the Highlands of Truro to the harbor of Chatham that the coastline at that time extended hundreds of feet further to the east than it does today. It is hard to imagine as one stands upon the cliffs and looks out over the waves, but those waves washed away unfathomable tons of earth,

earth upon which once stood lighthouses from centuries ago.

By 1892 the three brick lighthouses of Nauset crumbled into the sea to join their four Chatham cousins to the south. Three new, slightly taller wooden towers, known as the Three Sisters, were constructed on the Nauset cliff. It didn't take long for erosion to threaten these three beacons as well. In 1918 the north and south towers were spared, sold to become part of a cottage in Eastham. The middle tower stood alone atop the Nauset dune until 1923 when she too was sold to become part of another cottage in town.

That same year, the northernmost Chatham twin was dismantled and moved north where it was reconstructed to become the current Nauset Light. Since then it has been given alternating white and red beams to distinguish her from her cousins to the north and south. So, the beam from Nauset Light is, in actuality, that of one of the Chatham twins, transplanted amongst the swaying beach grass atop the Eastham cliff.

In recent years, both Highland and Nauset lights were moved back from their eroding cliffs, saved so that future generations may marvel at their magnificent beams.

Today we stare up in awe at Highland Light as if it were some ancient temple. A deep orange-red sun touches the southwestern horizon, signaling the end of another day. Billowing puffs of deep purple clouds over the ocean hurry along their way, pushed along by steady winds foretelling of an approaching storm.

Further south, twilight arrives at Nauset Beach. A white eye followed by a red eye scan the horizons, calling out their warning. Along Cable Road, just a few hundred yards west of the current Nauset Light, sit the Three Sisters in an opening in the woods, each one hundred and fifty feet apart as they sat upon a dune that no longer exists. In the departing light their dwarfed white forms appear as if three ghosts, the two on either end decapitated, only the one in the middle possessing the lantern room atop. In 1990 the three towers were brought back together, a family reunion of sorts, to form this touching historical exhibit.

South again, darkness, stars scattered above like grains of sand bow to the sweeping, silent beam of Chatham Light calling out some twenty-eight miles into the pitch. Now that the whole story

Chatham Lighthouse, originally a twin, now stands alone to cast her beam across the waves. (J. Sheedy photo)

is known, that there once were two towers here, it is easy to understand why the sight of the solitary tower standing to the left of the Coast Guard Station seems "unbalanced." Just imagine her twin on the other side, her beam also cutting through the darkness, balancing the picture.

At Nature's Mercy

Of Provincetown's three lighthouses, all three are still in operation today. Race Point's original twenty-five-foot lighthouse was built in 1816. It had a revolving light that was later changed to a flashing beam. A fog bell was installed that, in turn, was converted to a steam whistle. The tower was replaced in 1876 with the current iron and brick tower, possessing a fixed light resting some forty-one feet above the ocean waves.

At the Cape's last gasp of land marking the entrance to Provincetown Harbor rests Long Point Light. Though the present tower was built in 1875, the original light was constructed in 1827 atop the lighthouse keeper's house. From the 1820s to the 1840s a saltworks village existed in this locale with a couple of hundred residents calling the sandy terrain their home. But the community dried up as the salt making business crumbled. Today Long Point Light stands alone, solar panels now providing power for the light.

Resembling Long Point Light is the nearby Wood End Light. Like her cousin to the northeast, she is a square white tower capped with a black lantern room. Built on the site of two abandoned Civil War forts on the dunes of Provincetown, she was accompanied by a fog bell in 1902. Wood End, like Long Point, became an automated light with solar panels.

At Woods Hole, upon a bluff overlooking the dancing waves below, stands the proud Nobska Light. She was built in 1828 as an octagonal light tower atop the keeper's house. About fifty years later a fog bell was added. A free standing iron lighthouse some eighty-seven feet above the sea and painted red replaced the original Nobska Light in 1876. The current white tower is now automated, and has been since the mid-1980s.

The Mid-Cape's only operating lighthouse is Bass River Light, today residing above the Lighthouse Inn Restaurant at West Dennis Beach. This lighthouse was erected in 1855 to mark the entrance to Bass River, replacing a lantern in the window of a nearby house.

Bass River Light was shut down briefly from 1880 to 1881, but then remained in operation until the opening of the Cape Cod Canal in 1914. The beam was silenced once again, seemingly for good, and remained silent for three-quarters of a century until it was rekindled in 1989 with a new identity: West Dennis Light. Today she is a seasonal lighthouse, her light flashing forty-four feet above West Dennis Beach from May through October.

The town of Barnstable had two lighthouses during the age of sail, one on the northern beach and the other on the southern coastline. Both landmarks are still with us today.

First built was Sandy Neck Light, in 1827, at what was then the tip of Sandy Neck peninsula. At that time Barnstable Harbor was a busy northeast port and a lighthouse was deemed necessary to mark the harbor's entrance. The initial lighthouse consisted of a tower atop the keeper's house. At a height of thirty-three feet above sea level and a price tag of roughly $3,500, it cost the government just more than $100 for each elevated foot.

Exactly thirty years after its construction, the tower and house to which it was attached fell into such disrepair that a new lighthouse was built in its place. The current white tower was erected in 1857 and remained in service for three-quarters of a century. A new keeper's house was built in the 1880s. Today the house and tower are a private residence, existing with a colony of other cottages across the waters of Barnstable Harbor.

Meanwhile, South Hyannis Light was built in 1849 upon a bluff at the harbor entrance, replacing a primitive lighthouse in the form of a lantern in the window of an old shack. At twenty-one feet tall, it was considered the shortest lighthouse on the east coast. Her small frame stood between thirty and forty feet above sea level and utilized a system of oil lamps and reflectors to warn mariners of the rocks and shoals. After seven years the lamps were replaced with a Fresnel lens.

In 1885, a small square range light was added to aid mariners attempting to locate the harbor's entrance. The lighthouse remained active for eighty years and has since become a private residence.

Of the Cape's eighteen lighthouses, eleven were built along the Lower Cape from Provincetown to Monomoy. Of those remaining, five were put along the Mid-Cape coastlines, and only two at the Upper Cape. Their positioning was dictated by the flow of nineteenth century oceangoing traffic, also coinciding with the locations of the majority of wrecks over the centuries.

Six of the lighthouses still in operation today reside along the Lower Cape, still guarding that treacherous coastline. Much has changed since the last Cape lighthouse was built at Stage Harbor in 1880. As a species we have mastered the skies, even our small neighborhood of space. Yet, as far as we've traveled during the past century, a mariner on the sea at night upon a rocking ship amidst the stormy winter waves can still find comfort in seeing the beam from Highland Light.

Lighthouses fascinate us. Their light soothes us. One can now understand the companionship author-naturalist Henry Beston felt in seeing the beam of Nauset as he spent his year alone on the Eastham dune. It is a sight our ancestors saw atop these cliffs a century ago, and that we can still see today.

Lighthouses remind us that despite our many technological advances the sea is still a mightier being. Lighthouses remind us that, though we can send spacecraft to distant planets and send satellite messages around the globe in nanoseconds, the earth still rules us. And we must play by her rules.

Lighthouses, and the simple message carried with their beams, remind us that despite our many great strides we are still at nature's mercy upon the unforgiving waves of the great planet earth.

Bishop and Clerks' Light

About three miles south of Point Gammon off Great Island in West Yarmouth is a dangerous line of rocks that has long been a danger to mariners. Colonial records indicate that the area was once an island of almost five acres that for many years supported sheep grazing before the relentless tides and winter storms submerged the land sometime in the mid-eighteenth century. Left behind was a dangerous shoal and eight series of large rocks, one very large that was nicknamed "the Bishop," and the rest, his "Clerks."

In 1857 a solid stone lighthouse was built on large granite blocks brought out to the ledge. The structure was almost seventy feet high and flashed a white light accompanied by a warning bell every thirty seconds. The wooden structure that was attached to the light tower housed the bell and fog horn.

The light was situated to serve the maritime traffic that sailed the dangerous route through Nantucket Sound around Cape Cod in

For nearly one hundred years Bishop & Clerks' Lighthouse was a fixture in Nantucket Sound. (J. Coogan Collection)

the period before the Cape Cod Canal was built. In the late-nineteenth century, large numbers of coasting vessels used this sea highway to transfer cargoes of lumber, coal, ice, and salt fish to ports along the southern New England shore.

As the maritime fortunes of New England declined in the first years of the twentieth century, so also did the need to maintain the great number of navigation lights along the Cape Cod coastline. In 1928, the light was taken out of service and abandoned. After years of watching the structure disintegrate, and fearing that its continued presence might attract the curious day-sailing adventurer, the Coast Guard had the light destroyed in the fall of 1952. Today there is only a pyramid-shaped radar reflector on the site of the lighthouse to warn modern sailors of the still very real dangers of the waters around Bishop and Clerks' shoal.

Cross Rip, Nantucket & Vineyard Lightships

Throughout the latter half of the nineteenth century until beyond the mid-point of the twentieth century, a fleet of lightships marked the dangerous shoals around the Cape. The crews of these lightships balanced long hours and days of tediousness with frightful moments of sheer peril amidst stormy seas. As the tales of the *Cross Rip*, *Nantucket* and *Vineyard* lightships will attest, it was not all basket making!

During the fierce and frozen winter of 1918 four lightships were trapped by ice and ripped free from their anchors. Two lightships broke away from the ice to return to their stations. *Pollock Rip #47* was dragged by the ice floe all the way to Long Island. As for the fourth lightship, *Cross Rip #6*, hers is one of the Cape's saddest shipwreck stories.

In February of that year she became hopelessly iced in, making it impossible for ships to reach her. Her crew of six sat tight upon the sea of ice. The tale goes that a member of the crew was actually able to leave the vessel and walk across the ice field to land in order to ask permission to abandon the icebound lightship. Permission was denied, so out he walked back to his ship, and his doom.

Finally, the vessel was ripped free of her moorings and drifted around Nantucket Sound in sight of land for a number of days. Very soon, though, she drifted out of sight and was never heard from again. Fifteen years later wreckage was found in the waters off Nantucket believed to be from the *#6*.

The Nantucket station saw many mishaps. The very first lightship was wrecked in 1855 after only one year in service, about fifty miles off station. Her replacement wandered off station some twenty-five times, once reportedly blown eight hundred miles by a gale in October 1878. In 1892, the lightship stranded off Noman's Land. A relief vessel manning the station sank in a gale in 1905 and is considered the first American vessel to use the wireless to send a message of distress. Nearly thirty years later, #117 was rammed by the vessel *Washington* in January 1934, just four months prior to another collision that would send her to the bottom.

On May 15, 1934, the *Titanic's* sister ship, *Olympic*, was making what seemed like just another transatlantic run when she collided with the *Nantucket Lightship #117* in foggy conditions fifty miles southeast of Nantucket. Actually, "collide" does not accurately describe the encounter as the word implies two vessels of rather equal size bumping into each other. In this case, the nearly nine hundred-foot long, 45,000-ton *Olympic*, traveling at a meager sixteen knots because of the fog, dwarfed the 1,000-ton lightship. The *#117* sank almost immediately. Only the captain and three of his crew survived; four men died at the moment of collision while three others died later of the injuries they sustained.

The very next year the *Olympic* was retired. In 1936, the British presented the United States Coast Guard with a new lightship, *#112*, to replace the *#117*. *Nantucket Lightship #112* was later changed to *#534* and eventually became a floating lightship museum.

Yet, the greatest loss of life on a Cape Cod lightship occurred on September 14, 1944. A hurricane struck the Cape head on, and right in its path was the *Vineyard Lightship #73* and her crew of twelve.

Lightship #73 was built in 1901 and was initially stationed at Pollock Rip. She had three different names over a quarter century - *Pollock Rip Shoals*, *Pollock*, and *Slue*. In 1925 she was relocated to Buzzards Bay to replace *Vineyard Sound #90*. Her master in 1944 was Captain Edgar Sevigny.

Stationed at Sow and Pigs Reef off Cuttyhunk Island, #73 battled the greater than one hundred-mile-per-hour winds of the 1944 hurricane and in the end her storm anchor broke loose to ram her hull. Into the open wound poured the sea and down she went with her crew. Although bodies began to wash up on Cuttyhunk the following day, news of her loss was not released until four days later because, with the war on, the lightship held a strategic position near one end of the Cape Cod Canal.

Nineteen years later the wreckage of the lightship was discovered about twenty miles south of New Bedford in one hundred and twenty feet of water. The ship's bell was salvaged from the wreck and presented to the Coast Guard.

Her replacement was the former *Pollock Rip Lightship #110*. Ten years later, she was slammed by another hurricane and one of her crewmen was lost overboard. Fortunately, he was found alive on the very next day.

United States Lifesaving Stations

A gentle spring breeze greets the Atlantic waves as they spill
their walls of water upon the sands of Head of the Meadow Beach,
Truro. A tide low yet growing with each approaching wave rises
and falls around the wreck of the bark *Frances*, which collided with
these bars back on the evening of December 26, 1872.

Her blackened iron bones poke out of the water so close to shore
that it seems one could easily wade out to the wreck. Yet to her
crewmen a century and a quarter ago the shoreline must have
seemed miles and miles away. Upon that December evening all
hands were saved by Captain Edwin Worthen and a crew of
volunteers who hauled a boat from the bay side to the ocean side
of Truro to make the rescue. Worthen was the new keeper of the
Highland lifesaving station then under construction.

Captain Wilhelm Kortling of the one hundred and twenty-foot
Frances was ill for the few weeks leading up to the wreck, and died
three days after the rescue. So moved was Captain Worthen that
for more than a quarter century he looked after Kortling's Truro
grave. Two men, each unknown to the other, yet they became
forever linked by the events of that stormy December eve off Head
of the Meadow Beach.

In the years that straddled the turn of the century, before the Cape
Cod Canal was built, in the times when shipwrecks frequented the
outer Cape shore, a legion of surfmen would patrol the dark shores
of night with one eye on the dunes and one eye on the seas.

For a span of forty-three years this patrol guarded the Lower
Cape beaches, forty-three years of winters, forty-three years of
blizzards and hurricanes and nor'easters. For forty-three years
Cape surfmen battled with the shoals and bars of Race Point,
Peaked Hill Bars, Pamet River, Nauset ... and Monomoy. For forty-
three years shipwrecked sailors caught in the web of a watery
grave were snatched from the hereafter and cast upon the shore
like Jonah cast forth from the belly of the whale.

To trace the beginnings of the Lifesaving Service of Cape Cod

A Nauset USLSS surfboat now at the Old Harbor Station in Provincetown. (J. Sheedy photo)

one must look back to the Massachusetts Humane Society. Formulated in 1786, it is considered the first such society in the country to assist shipwreck survivors. The society built ninety-two small refuge huts along the coastline at locations prone to wrecks, providing victims fortunate enough to make it to shore shelter from the elements until help could arrive.

The United States government realized the need for a service to assist shipwrecked mariners and in 1847 allocated money toward that purpose. Although the intention was good, the plan failed miserably. The stations built were too few and far between to do any good and were manned by inexperienced persons who lacked the necessary disciplines. The stations suffered from theft and quickly fell into disrepair.

In 1872, the government came back with a new plan, thus establishing the United States Life Saving Service (USLSS), building nine such stations on Cape Cod. This new plan involved the hiring of a keeper and a team of paid surfmen for each station rather than volunteers as with the earlier plan. The keepers were paid $200 per year in 1872, which eventually increased to $900 by the turn of the century. Meanwhile, surfmen were hired on a year-to-year basis.

The keeper, who had to be a "man of good character" between the ages of twenty-one and forty-five, in good physical shape and an expert boatman, lived at the station year round. The surfmen of the station were assigned from August 1 until June 1 of the following year. They worked six days a week with Sundays off. These surfmen were ranked according to their experience, with Surfman Number 1 being the highest rank and the most likely candidate to replace the keeper upon his retirement, disability or death.

Each year the surfmen needed to pass a physical exam. If he were to become injured in the line of duty to the point where he could not work he would receive his pay for one year. If he were to give the supreme sacrifice his widow would be entitled to two years' pay.

The stations themselves were built so as to be between three and five miles apart. The nine original stations built in 1872 were placed at Race Point and Peaked Hill Bars in Provincetown, Highlands and Pamet River in Truro, Cahoon's Hollow in Wellfleet, Nauset in Eastham, Orleans, Chatham and on Monomoy. They were later joined by four other stations: Wood End at Provincetown in 1897, High Head at Truro in 1883, Old Harbor at Chatham in 1898 and at Monomoy Point in 1902.

The typical layout of a three-story station included a kitchen, mess, keeper's room and the large boat and beach apparatus room on the lower level. Crew sleeping quarters and a storeroom, which doubled as a wreck survivors sleeping quarters, were on the second level. On the third level was an observation tower. The boat and beach apparatus room contained two surfboats and perhaps a dory, carriages to transport the boats to the wreck location, two sets of breeches buoy and carts to carry the apparatus down to the beach.

The Lower Cape coastline was a busy route in the days before the canal. From the observation tower of each station the watchman on duty would log the flow of traffic. From the flagstaff setup outside the station the crew could communicate with passing ships and by wire would be able to pass news down the line to the other twelve stations, or inland if necessary.

The work week began at midnight on Sunday. Each day held a

On display at the Old Harbor Station is a beach cart and breeches buoy used to rescue shipwrecked mariners. (J. Sheedy photo)

different task. On Mondays the crew cleaned up around the station and made sure all equipment was in working order. Tuesdays saw lifeboat drills, which included launching the boat into the surf and righting a capsized boat. On Wednesdays the crew was drilled in the use of the international and general signal codes used to communicate via the flagstaff with ships at sea. Thursdays brought the breeches buoy apparatus out of the station for drills on the beach. A good crew could have the system operational in five minutes. First aid drilling was done on Fridays, while Saturdays were reserved as wash day.

And at night, every night regardless of the weather, the surfmen walked the beaches. The watches ran from sunset to 8 p.m., from 8 p.m. to midnight, midnight to 4 a.m., and from 4 a.m. until sunrise. The surfmen would start out from their station, one walking north and the other south along the shore for about two and a half miles until he reached either a halfway hut or a designated ending point. There he would meet the surfman from the neighboring station. They might exchange information and then the surfmen would travel back to their stations. In this way, the entire length of the Cape from Wood End to Monomoy Point was monitored through-out the night, every night, from dusk till dawn.

The surfmen would carry a Coston signal and if a wreck was sighted he would ignite the flare to signal the ship that help was on the way. The crew of the station would be mustered. Depending upon the location of the wreck and the weather conditions, it would be decided the best mode of rescue. There were essentially two methods, one by land and one by sea.

If the wreck lay well offshore a surfboat would be launched. This was not an easy feat. Imagine dragging a twenty-four foot long, one thousand-pound boat in a cart across miles of sand, down dune cliffs, in pitch darkness, and in wind or rain or snow. And that was just to get the boat down to the shoreline!

Then imagine launching this craft into an angry sea of huge winter waves, along a coastline boasting fierce undertows, into the very icy fury that has, by its very makeup, claimed a two-hundred-foot vessel now breaking up on the bars ahead. At any time a crewman could tumble into the dark sea and be lost, or a surfboat could become capsized, or crushed by the bulk of the wrecked vessel as it lurched with the gigantic waves. It seems an impossible task.

If the seas were too rough to successfully launch a boat, or if the wreck was close enough to the shore, the breeches buoy would be employed. This was an ingenious system that created in a matter of minutes a pulley system between the ship and shore over which shipwreck victims could be transported.

A Lyle gun, which resembled a little cannon, would fire an eighteen-pound shot hundreds of yards through the air and into the rigging of the wrecked ship. A crewman on the wreck would climb up into the rigging and retrieve the line carried by the shot. Once done, ropes would be hauled over to the crippled vessel and fastened to a mast until the apparatus was in place and operational. The breeches buoy, so-called because it resembled a pair of canvas breeches with a buoyant tube at the waist, would be hauled over to the ship and one by one the crewmen would be taken off in it.

In his book *Surfmen and Lifesavers*, Paul Giambarba states that between 1872 and 1915 some ninety-nine percent of all those involved in shipwrecks along the coastlines of the country serviced by US lifesaving stations were saved, some 177,000 people in total.

The Lower Cape coastline is littered with wrecks, and though many mariners were lost even with the establishment of the thirteen stations on Cape, many, many more were saved who would otherwise have perished. During its first decade of operation, about one hundred and seventy vessels wrecked along the Cape coast guarded by the USLSS. Only twenty-one of the estimated 1,250 people involved in these wrecks perished.

The building of the Cape Cod Canal in 1914, and the development of safer steel-hulled ships powered by propeller rather than by wind and canvas, meant a drastic reduction in the numbers of wrecks along the outer Cape. By 1915 the lifesaving service on Cape Cod outlived its purpose and was combined with the Revenue Cutter Service to become the US Coast Guard, a new agency formed during that same year.

At Race Point, at what can be considered the very ends of the earth, is the Old Harbor Lifesaving Station that once rested at Chatham. Decommissioned in 1944 after forty-six years of service, it was purchased in 1946 to become a private cottage. In 1973 the National Park Service acquired it and with the beach eroding, dismantled and moved it via ocean to Provincetown in 1977. Surviving the Blizzard of 1978 while resting on a barge in Provincetown Harbor, it was put in place at Race Point later that year to become a lifesaving museum, the entire move costing about $1 million.

Walking through the rooms of the building one cannot help but see the ghosts of surfmen and the survivors they pulled from the sea. Each room echoes with their voices, each floorboard creaks with their footsteps.

The walls are painted an institutional olive green. The stairs are steep and narrow. On the main floor are a number of rooms, including the keeper's chamber. Upstairs is the dormitory with windows overlooking the sand and the surf. Though the room is empty, one can envision cots and duffel bags arranged in an orderly fashion. Above this second floor, via a wooden ladder, is the lookout tower. It is a square room, about eight feet by eight. The height gives one a commanding view of the beach and the sea beyond. But a breeze at ground level, the wind at this height howls and moans, speaking in a voice that only surfmen and ship-wrecked mariners can understand fully.

Down below, on the main level, is the boat room. Inside is a beach cart to haul the lifesaving apparatus, a boat cart, a twenty-four-foot long surfboat, and a smaller Coast Guard dory. The station's old log book survives to this day; the cover reads "Wreck Report, Old Harbor Life Saving Station, District No. 2, May 24, 1898 through August 14, 1913." Inside are handwritten notes of disasters now part of Cape legend and lore.

Greater than three-quarters of a century has passed since the last entry was made in the Old Harbor log. Those days seem so distant. Yet, one need only hear the thunderous crash of a wave upon Head of the Meadow Beach to be reminded of the times when ships wrecked and brave men rowed through the tempest in the hopes of bringing back a survivor.

And one need only see the wreck of the *Francis* with her black-ened skeletal remains reaching above the waves to remember a particular night in December 1872 when her crew and a handful of Cape volunteers did battle with nature, and won.

Captain Mayo - Wrecker, Anchor Dragger, Hero

Upon a peninsula brimming with stories of men doing battle with the sea, the story of the brave men who participated in the Monomoy Disaster will forever be remembered. Nearly a century later it still commands our attention, as it rightly should, for contained within the morning of March 17, 1902 was a drama transcending generations.

Nearby Chatham Light, upon a cliff overlooking surf always treacherous, is a monument that relates the story of that fateful March day. Chiseled upon the stone are the names and the deeds that linked the land mass Monomoy and the word "disaster" so thoroughly for Cape Codders who study and worship this Lower Cape coastline and the brave men who fought against it despite the odds.

With the roar of the sea accenting the chiseled words, one reads:

"In memory of the hero of the Monomoy Disaster, Capt. Elmer F. Mayo, Chatham, MA, and his gallant rescue of Surfman Seth L. Ellis from a watery grave on Shovelful Shoals off Monomoy Point, March 17, 1902."

Fifteen men were involved in the events of that March morning: twelve who perished, two who survived and one on the beach who helped land those two survivors. Widows would mourn, children would become fatherless, Cape Codders would hold vigils, and the two survivors would be hailed as heroes who willingly put their lives in harm's way at even the slightest chance of saving the life of another.

Captain Seth Ellis was born October 12, 1858, the son of a sea captain by the same name. At the tender age of nine he went to sea with his father. By the age of fifteen he was a mackerel fisherman. In his late teens he survived the wreck of the vessel *Enos B. Phillips,* which was ripped apart during a blizzard. Realizing the changing times from the days of wooden sailing ships to more contemporary vessels, he later became a steamboat captain.

A skilled boatman, he joined the ranks at Monomoy lifesaving station in 1895, eventually being promoted to Surfman Number 1 by 1902 under the command of keeper Captain Marshall Eldredge. His skills would be put to the ultimate test on that March morning.

There was a fog clinging to the waves off Monomoy Island. Off shore, two barges lay on Shovelful Shoals where they became stranded on March 11 after breaking away from the tug *Peter Smith.* The crews of both barges, the *Wadena* and the *Fitzpatrick,* were taken ashore earlier by the skilled surfmen of Captain Eldredge's Monomoy Station. Wrecking crews were now on both vessels attempting to lighten their cargoes so they might be floated off the shoals. Most of the wreckers of both barges came ashore on the evening of March 16 because of bad weather and rough seas. The crew at the Monomoy Lifesaving Station assumed that all the wreckers left the barges, so they were surprised the next morning to see a distress signal fluttering from the rigging of the *Wadena.*

From the shore, the crew of the station did not detect any signs of distress, but the code of the lifesaving service was simply put: "You must go out!" So out they went, Captain Eldredge, Surfman Ellis and six other members of the station crew.

Through the rough waters of a gale they rowed out to the barge. The rips in this area are considered the most treacherous along the Cape shoreline, yet the lifesaving crew was successful in their attempt to reach the *Wadena*. They pulled up to the leeward side and took off the crew of five. On the way back toward shore is when disaster struck. A large wave engulfed the surfboat. The lifesaving crew continued to row despite the swamped condition of the boat, following Captain Eldredge's orders to the letter, according to the testimony of Surfman Ellis.

The wreckers, on the other hand, panicked and in their state of panic managed to capsize the boat.

One by one, the men in the water drowned under the relentless waves, first the five wreckers and then the lifesavers as they twice righted the surfboat in rough seas only to have the waves capsize it for a third and final time. In the end, Number 1 Surfman Ellis alone remained alive, clinging to the centerboard of the capsized boat, his comrades and captain drowned. Fatigued by his earlier attempts to right the boat, he could do nothing but hang on for as long as his strength would allow.

Meanwhile, across the waters, Captain Elmer F. Mayo on the other grounded barge, *Fitzpatrick*, noticed a capsized surfboat bobbing and disappearing again with the high seas and the drifting fog. He then noticed a lone surfman clinging to the boat. Mayo knew from his stints as a Cape lifesaver that a surfboat typically carried a crew of seven, so the magnitude of the disaster at hand became quite evident.

Without a thought for his own safety, and against the pleas of those others aboard the *Fitzpatrick*, Mayo quickly stripped to his underwear, climbed down a rope and with only a fourteen-foot dory between himself and a watery grave rowed out to the surfman on the capsized boat.

Mayo, born in 1862 at Chatham, was a well-known Cape wrecker and anchor dragger and was considered an expert boatman. His father was a lifesaving station keeper at Chatham and he himself was a substitute lifesaver from time to time so he knew his way around a surfboat and breeches buoy.

In his vessel *Wilfred W. Fuller*, Mayo would anchor drag with his

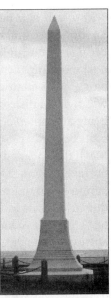

This Chatham monument, overlooking Shovelful Shoal, remembers those who perished in the Monomoy Disaster, as well as the two surviving heroes – Captain Elmer Mayo and Surfman Seth Ellis. (J. Sheedy photos)

partner Ralph Hunter, also of Chatham. Hunter would pilot the ship while Mayo would stand in the cross trees and search the sandy bottom below for lost anchors. Using various retrieval apparatus, some of which Mayo invented himself, he and Hunter would haul up their finds. One anchor he retrieved, from the vessel *Asia*, weighed 4,500 pounds and sold in Boston for five cents a pound. The anchor chain, at one hundred and eighty fathoms (roughly one thousand feet), brought three cents per pound. In those days, such a find was equal to half a year's salary. Needless to say, with all the ships losing anchors and chains around the Cape a skilled anchor dragger could make a good living.

Mayo was also a skilled wrecker. In his schooner *Gleaner* he would comb the shoals for sunken wrecks to see what treasures they held. Wrecks could offer any number of things, from fishing nets to canvas sails, and from navigational equipment to cleats and blocks and even rope. And of course, there was always the cargo the ship carried.

In March 1902 he was hired to refloat the barge *Fitzpatrick*. Though most of the wrecking crew went ashore on March 16 because of the high seas, he and a small crew stayed on board. The next morning, the fog was so thick that he could not see the other barge, *Wadena*, stranded on the same shoal and did not know she was flying a distress signal. He was also unaware of the rescue being attempted across the waters.

Successfully plucking the exhausted Ellis from certain death, Mayo then headed the dory toward shore. On the beach was Surfman Bloomer who did not accompany his comrades on the surfboat that morning merely because it was his day for kitchen duty. He noticed the dory plunging toward shore. It was not until he helped Mayo land the boat that he learned of the tragedy. By attrition Bloomer would move up to Surfman Number 1, and Ellis would be promoted to keeper of the Monomoy station.

For his "acts of extreme heroism" Mayo would receive citations from the Massachusetts Human Society and the United States Government. Afterwards he returned to his life as a wrecker. Later he left Cape Cod, first going to the Klondike in search of gold, then to Seattle to do some deep sea fishing. For a time he was a fisherman down in the south. As old age met him he returned to Chatham to live out the last years of his life. He died in the summer of 1935, the same year as fellow Monomoy hero Seth Ellis. The drama that took place upon the waves of Shovelful Shoals had ended.

Today, ten decades later, a countless number of waves have curled over these shoals only to crash upon this outer Cape shoreline, their contribution to the grand celestial plan completed with their waters rushing upon the flat and ocean worn sands. So many waves, so many years.

How safe we are on dry land, how utterly secure in our notion that we control this planet. But we are mistaken if we are to underestimate her immense power. Twelve men in a surfboat were no match for the unforgiving waves. And yet two men alone survived these very same waters to tell the tale of what Cape Codders call with a true Yankee pride the Monomoy Disaster.

Chapter 6

Cape Codders at War

This narrow peninsula can point to a proud history of defending our country against enemy attack.

From the Colonial War to the Gulf War, Cape Codders answered the call. In the mid-eighteenth century, the inspirational words of West Barnstable born Patriot James Otis, Jr. gave birth to this country. In the Revolutionary War to follow, the British bombarded Cape towns and seized Cape ships. The boys of Falmouth took on the Brits after withstanding cannon fire on their town, and remarkably, they were victorious.

With the War of 1812, the British returned to this land thrust out unprotected into the sea, sending their cannonballs once again toward Falmouth. And once again, the Falmouth militia got the better of the Brits. Along the Lower Cape, the Orleans militia also took on the Royal Navy in what became known as the Battle of Rock Harbor. A little more than a century later Orleans would be attacked again, this time by a German U-boat during World War I.

James Otis ~ The First Patriot

The Otis family of eighteenth century Barnstable holds a special place in the history books. Their influence was felt not only on Cape Cod and in Massachusetts, but throughout the colonies and clear across the ocean to Great Britain.

Colonel James Otis was a General Court representative and Governor's Councilor during the years leading up to the Revolutionary War. His grandfather, John Otis, arrived at Great Marshes, now West Barnstable, in 1667 and was able to trace his ancestry back to Barnstaple, England - the namesake of Barnstable, Massachusetts. Colonel Otis and his wife Mary Allyne Otis went on to have thirteen children (many of them did not live past childhood), a number of them playing important roles during the decades before, during and after the American Revolution.

Daughter Mercy Otis Warren became a political satirist, using her pen to poke fun at the crown through poetry and plays. Her three volume history of the Revolutionary War was the first such work written by an American. The Colonel's son, Joseph, was a general in the Revolutionary War and was known for his quick temper and, at times, wild behavior. Another son, Samuel Allyne Otis, became Secretary of State and actually held the Bible when George Washington took his first oath of office in 1789.

But it was son James, Jr. who led the pack. He was, perhaps, America's first Patriot - before Samuel Adams, before John Hancock, before Patrick Henry, before them all. In fact, so substantial was his contribution to the cause of the revolution that he has been forever honored with the most appropriate title, "the Patriot."

James Otis, Jr. was born on February 5, 1725 at West Barnstable. A plaque on a boulder along Route 6A, midway between routes 132 and 149, marks the location of the Otis homestead where James "first saw the light." Otis graduated from Harvard in 1743, earning his master's degree in 1746. Deciding that he wanted to be a lawyer, he studied law for the next two years and began his practice in 1748, first in Barnstable and later in Plymouth. In 1750 he relocated to Boston.

In 1755, after establishing a successful law practice, Otis married

James Otis, Jr. monument in front of the Barnstable County Courthouse in Barnstable Village. (J. Sheedy photo)

Ruth Cunningham, the daughter of a Boston businessman. In the years to follow, it would be Otis' fight for the cause of the colonial merchants that would elevate him to prominence and make his name synonymous with the term "Patriot."

By 1760, Otis earned the position of Advocate General of the Vice Admiralty Court, for which he was paid handsomely. This position saw him upholding British rule, and over time Otis felt his lofty position was in direct conflict with all in which he believed. Though he sided with the cause of the Boston merchants, his role as Advocate General assisted the British in stifling the merchants' freedoms. By early 1761 the spark of freedom flickered to life.

It all started with the death of King George II in 1760. As was normally done when a new king was crowned, the writs of the empire were renewed. So it was when George III took the throne. The Writs of Assistance were tightened like a noose around the colonists' neck, and as Advocate General it was Otis' job to defend them. Instead, Otis resigned his position, thereby forfeiting his generous salary, to oppose the writs as counsel for the Boston merchants. The Advocate General became the Brits' adversary!

The new Writs of Assistance were rewritten in an attempt to put further pressures on the colonies. The Brits suspected the colonists of violating the Navigational Acts, of smuggling illegal cargoes into the colonies and of trading with the enemy during the French and Indian War. The Writs would make it legal for private homes, businesses and even ships at sea to be searched by customs officers at any time for any reason without a warrant.

In February 1761, Otis delivered his famous speech against the Writs of Assistance in the council chamber at Boston's Old State House. He spoke for four hours before a panel of judges including Lieutenant Governor Thomas Hutchinson, and in those four hours lit the spark of revolution in the hearts of his compatriots. John Adams, who was present when Otis delivered his speech, later wrote: "Mr. Otis' oration breathed into this nation the breath of life ... then and there was the first scene of the first act of the opposition to the arbitrary claims of Great Britain ... American independence was then and there born."

In his speech Otis argued that the British writs were unconstitutional. But his arguments transcended the issues of common law. He maintained that the writs were in violation of natural law, elevating the issues at hand to political and philosophical levels. He even spoke of human rights and used the speech to denounce slavery.

Though no copies of the speech survived, those present described it as "eloquent," "impassioned," "momentous," and the product of "conclusive reasoning." Adams did happen to take some notes during the speech and sixty years later attempted to reconstruct what he could of Otis' oration. He later said "Otis was a flame of fire" and that he had "a prophetic glance of his eyes into futurity." Otis even made reference to "my country" when referring to the colonies, marking the first instance of anyone conceiving of a nation separate and independent from the crown.

The speech against the Writs of Assistance was the conception of the whole notion of the Boston Patriot and launched a suspicion of the British that never faded. From that time forward, British rule was always questioned and scrutinized.

Meanwhile, Otis emerged as a self-confident speaker with a genius that was balanced by a burning anger ... an infectious burning anger. His message and philosophies unleashed during those four historic hours at the State House escaped out into the streets and taverns of Boston. Over the weeks and months to follow, it spread like wildfire to the streets of New York and Philadelphia, giving birth to patriotism and planting the very seeds of revolution. The Brits didn't stand a chance of maintaining their grasp on the free-thinking colonists.

Otis became a nationally recognized patriot, statesman, pamphleteer and orator. He was elected to the General Court in 1761 as a representative from Boston and five years later was elected speaker although the royal governor disallowed his appointment due to his strong anti-British stance and his position concerning the Stamp Act.

In 1764 he voiced his opposition to the Sugar Act by stating that "no parts of his Majesty's domain can be taxed without their consent." The following year he was one of the major colonial figures at the Stamp Act Congress of 1765, while he decried the Townshend Act in 1767 by writing that "no one should be taxed without representation." He wrote a number of pamphlets and letters from 1764 to 1768 protesting British rule, some co-authored by other Boston Patriots including Samuel Adams.

By the later years of the 1760s his angry verbal attacks on the British were becoming dangerously potent. He made many enemies over the years, and a handful of these enemies made their presence known in September 1769. Otis was severely beaten by a group of British customs officials at the British Coffee House on State Street in Boston. Though he survived the attack, his skull was fractured and damage to his brain became abundantly evident. For the remainder of his life he would battle for his sanity. Much of the time his mental condition was shattered, his sense of reasoning destroyed, and yet he would have periods of lucid behavior reminding those around him of his younger days of fire and flame at Boston's State House. But it was not to be. His lucidity would regress back to lunacy.

Though he was awarded £2,000 in damages and received a written apology from the commissioner of customs, it would not help to repair the destruction done to Otis' mental state. In 1770 he literally went mad at the State House, breaking windows, burning his papers and firing off a rifle. He was judged a lunatic and his brother, Samuel, was named his guardian. Despite his condition, he actually served briefly in the legislature during 1771, but by then he was merely a shell of his former self.

Afterwards, he was removed to Lawrence Pond in Sandwich to stay at the home of family friend Joseph Lawrence. Lawrence agreed to watch over the former Patriot and orator. Yet, on a number of occasions Otis would be found missing only to turn up somewhere along the carriage route between Barnstable and Boston, his damaged mind probably telling him that he had speeches to deliver at the State House and pamphlets to write at his downtown office.

Upon one such disappearance, on June 17, 1775 to be precise, Otis lifted a rifle from his sister Mercy's house in Watertown and wound up at the Battle of Bunker Hill! He survived the battle unharmed. Two years later, though, his own son James would die as a prisoner on board a British ship.

In the early 1780s he was relocated to the farm of Isaac Osgood in Andover, Massachusetts. He would spend the final two years of his life at the farm, living in a private apartment on the grounds.

On May 23, 1783, he was outside speaking to a small group of people who gathered to hear the "master," as John Adams later called him, recount stories of the pre-Revolutionary years. While he spoke, a storm blew in across the fields. Out of the sky came a bolt of lightning, striking the Patriot and killing him instantly. The great orator was finally silenced.

Because Otis' papers were destroyed and the contents of his speeches forever lost, his memory eluded the fame bestowed upon Patriots John and Samuel Adams, John Hancock, Paul Revere and Patrick Henry. His injuries in 1769 kept him from participating in the events of the 1770s leading up to the Declaration of Independence and war to follow. Yet, Otis was one of the central characters in our country's battle for independence. He was there at the very beginning. In fact, one could argue that Otis was the very beginning, a decade and a half before the Declaration of Independence, a document under which his signature would likely have appeared.

A little more than three months after Otis' death, the Treaty of Paris was signed between the newly formed United States and Great Britain. The revolution that James Otis began twenty-two years earlier was finally won.

The American Revolution's Feminine Pen

Any mention of the American Revolution as it relates to Cape Cod rightly includes the work and influence of James Otis, Jr. of Barnstable. Known as "The Patriot" by his contemporaries, Otis was heralded in the early stages of the independence movement for his fiery anti-British speeches. Many characterized him as the "northern Patrick Henry" in his strong stand against the infamous Writs of Assistance.

Only more recently has Otis' sister, Mercy Otis Warren been given recognition as playing a significant role in the struggle for liberty as both a writer of political satire and a confidant of a number of important Revolutionary personalities. Indeed, she is not even mentioned in Henry C. Kittredge's *Cape Cod: Its People and Their History*, the area's most widely quoted historical account. Yet her plays, comedies, and essays, often written anonymously as was the

style of the day, can be viewed as a feminine version of what the
more famous Thomas Paine was doing with his essays on liberty.

Mercy Otis was born in Barnstable on September 25, 1728 to an
upper middle class merchant family. Her father, Pilgrim descendant James Otis, Sr., was a well to do merchant of some political
and economic note in the colony. The elder Otis served as a member of the colonial Governor's Council. As such, the Otis house-
hold was often the scene of political discussion and interest in
affairs beyond the local community.

One of thirteen children, Mercy was perhaps closest in temperament to her older brother James. Although never formally schooled,
she nevertheless developed an interest in reading and her tastes
tended toward the classics and world issues. When her brother went
off to Harvard, she continued a lively correspondence with him and
in 1754 she married one of his classmates, the Plymouth aristocrat
and Mayflower descendant James Warren. This marriage lasted
fifty-four years and produced five sons. Although her husband
served in a number of official posts during the Revolutionary War, it
was Mercy who became the more well-known and self-anointed
feminine conscience of the independence movement.

When her brother James was beaten by Loyalists in 1769, effec-
tively removing him as an active spokesman for those who wanted
to break with England, Mercy began writing anti-Tory pamphlets
and poems that were published in weekly Patriot papers such as
the *Massachusetts Spy* and the *Boston Gazette*.

As a satirist, her work lampooned the area Loyalists with
stinging force. Her plays and melodramas cast thinly disguised
leading members of the Boston Loyalist community as ruffians and
buffoons and were outrageous in their criticism of the British
political administration of the colony. Her works were designed as
revolutionary propaganda and were widely read and appreciated
by men and women who favored independence.

Not so much a pure feminist as she was a champion of colonial
liberty, she cut across gender lines in calling for an end to British
political authority while urging women to actively boycott British
goods. Even though she clearly believed that a woman's intellect
could be equal to that of men, she wrote consistently that she

This plaque on a boulder along Route 6A in West Barnstable marks the birthplace of James Otis, Jr. and his sister Mercy who penned political satire during the period of the Revolutionary War. (J. Sheedy photo)

considered a woman's role of domestic helpmate as being a higher calling. But at least in some sense she must be considered at least a proto-feminist. As her husband conceded, "She has a woman's temperament, but a man's mind."

In 1790, all of her plays were published with her name boldly printed on them and she enjoyed wide readership. It was in these post-war years that Mercy Otis Warren began to establish herself politically as a strong republican in the Jeffersonian sense. She opposed the centralized power structure that came with the 1789 Constitution because she feared that it could allow a despotic leader to seize control of the new nation. This put her at odds with many of her former Massachusetts Patriot contemporaries who were staunch Federalists. Where she was formerly close to people like John Hancock, Samuel Adams, and John Adams, she now found herself being criticized by these proponents of a more centralized system of governmental authority.

In contrast to his early praise of her wartime literary effort, Adams referred to one of her later works as being "like mustard after dinner." Much of his criticism was directed at her 1805 three-volume publication of the first history of the Revolution entitled: *The History of the Rise, Progress, and Termination of the American Revolution*. The book, which covered the time from the Stamp Act controversy to the beginning of the nineteenth century, contained a good deal of anti-Federalist criticism, much of it directed at the second president's recently concluded administration and Adams never fully forgave her for it.

Eventually, in her final years, there was a rapprochement with many of her political adversaries, including Adams. She continued to correspond about the issues of the day with people she knew for more than half a century.

She finished her days in Plymouth, outliving her husband by six years, passing away at the age of eighty-four in October of 1814. As a crusader for liberty, Mercy Otis Warren demonstrated in her own special way that in a political struggle, the pen can certainly be as mighty as the sword.

Cape Cod's Military Encounters

During the American Revolutionary War and the War of 1812, Cape Cod's unique position some forty miles out to sea left her exposed to enemy attack. Her ports were blockaded, her ships were seized, her crops and livestock were stolen, and in some cases her towns were bombarded.

Cape Codders had two choices available to them, either give the British what they wanted or else put up a defense and fight them off. Many towns chose the former to avoid having their property destroyed. A smaller number took their chances with resistance. One of the towns to put up a fight, in both wars, was Falmouth. The town seemed constantly at odds with the Royal Navy and regularly fired on British ships passing along the coast. Their dislike of the British ran deep.

Falmouth was fortunate to have two strong leaders during both wars who not only put forth a resistance but actually beat the Brits each time at their own game. During the Revolutionary War that man was Colonel Joseph Dimmick. His War of 1812 counterpart was Captain Weston Jenkins. Each one went up against the great-

This cannon, now on display at Barnstable County Courthouse, was installed at Barnstable during the War of 1812 to save the village's salt works from British attack. (J. Sheedy photo)

est navy in the world, and was victorious.

On April 2, 1779, the British fleet landed at Falmouth. As was the theme during wartime, they were coming ashore to steal provisions, in this particular case the prize being cattle. The local militia arrived on the scene and drove the marauders back to their base at Tarpaulin Cove on Naushon Island.

That night, at a Naushon tavern owned by Tory John Slocum, the British made plans to have their revenge on Falmouth the next day by burning the town. Slocum, overhearing the conversations, had a change of allegiance and sent his son across Vineyard Sound in a dory to warn Colonel Dimmick of the Falmouth militia. Dimmick's men dug entrenchments along the beach and readied themselves for attack.

Two British schooners and eight sloops appeared off the coast on the morning of April 3 to bombard Falmouth. Some two hundred and twenty British soldiers attempted to make landfall as cannonballs flew overhead from late morning to late afternoon, yet an army of Falmouth men held them off. The soft spring ground saturated by earlier rains swallowed many of the cannonballs.

Dimmick called for reinforcements from neighboring towns and men from Sandwich later joined his forces. Militia from Barnstable were on their way but received a message that they were no longer needed. The British withdrew to attempt a landing further west at Woods Hole but without success as Dimmick sent forces to protect the beach. Frustrated, the enemy went off to pillage the islands.

After the April 3 encounter with the British, Colonel Dimmick decided to go on the offensive. In a midnight meeting he drew up plans to win back a Falmouth schooner full of corn stolen by the Brits. The captain of the schooner escaped and informed Dimmick of the situation. At that time a schooner full of food was especially valuable as Cape ports were blocked and Cape towns were being pillaged to feed the British forces.

That morning, before daybreak, Dimmick took three whaleboats full of Falmouth militia into Tarpaulin Cove where they came upon the British fleet. With the light of sunrise they approached the hijacked schooner. The British fired upon the whaleboats. The Falmouth men answered with gunfire of their own. The men from Falmouth boarded the schooner yet in the confusion of battle ran her aground. They waited for high tide so the vessel could be set free, all the while successfully fighting off the British. Victorious, they sailed their schooner back to Woods Hole.

Later, Dimmick took a crew of twenty-five men to Vineyard Haven Harbor. Under the veil of darkness, he and his army engaged the British schooner *General Leslie*. Although the British ship out-gunned and out-manned him, Dimmick was successful in capturing the vessel, sailing her back to Hyannis along with a number of British prisoners he captured in the process.

Three decades later the British returned to Falmouth with the War of 1812 raging. Captain Weston Jenkins had earlier organized the Falmouth Artillery Company, so when the Brits arrived in January 1814 the men of Falmouth were ready for them.

It all began when the Falmouth Artillery detained a Nantucket sloop. The men of Falmouth suspected the Nantucketers of sympathizing with the British and therefore felt justified in taking their "Tory" vessel. The captain of the British brig *Nimrod* demanded that the Falmouth men release the ship, and while they were at it, that they also hand over the town's two brass cannons that the Falmouth militia were using to fire on passing British ships. Captain Jenkins refused to comply, telling the Brits to "Come and get 'em!" The British responded that the residents of Falmouth would be given two hours to evacuate before they proceeded with a bombardment of the town.

A large number of Falmouth residents vacated their homes, leaving the Falmouth military to fend off the enemy. At 10 a.m. on January 23 the *Nimrod's* eighteen cannons unleashed their attack, sending cannonballs flying into the village center. The minister's home was damaged, as was the church. In another house, Ann Freeman was cooking a meal for the Falmouth militia when a cannonball came through one of the walls and landed in a bed sending feathers flying. That house is today the Elm Arch Inn. Another cannonball took out the front door to Ichabod Hatch's house, another hit Elijah Swift's house. Swift would survive the attack to found the Falmouth National Bank eight years later.

The British did not attempt a landing, although the Falmouth militia was dug in on the beach just in case. Unable to score any major hits on Falmouth, the British sailed west to lob some cannonballs at Nobska Point. In their wake they left only one Falmouth home destroyed and some saltworks along the shore damaged. The rest of the town escaped with minor bruises and the people returned to their homes.

Like Colonel Dimmick from the earlier war, Captain Jenkins decided to take matters into his own hands. In a sloop named *Two Friends*, he sailed thirty-two volunteers off Woods Hole to engage the British ship *Retaliation*. Jenkins' plan was simple. He had thirty-one of his men hide below while he and one other man stood above to await the British soldiers who would, no doubt, pull up in a boat from the *Retaliation*. The Brits would consider the sloop, manned by only two, an easy prize. Then the army of Falmouth men would rise up and take the British by surprise.

It worked just as planned. Jenkins and his men took the *Retaliation* along with their British prisoners. An added bonus was the discovery of two American prisoners onboard the vessel. The *Retaliation* was sold, the cargo was given to the people of Falmouth and the British soldiers were marched to Boston.

Meanwhile, the people of Orleans were having their own problems with the British during the War of 1812. Falmouth had the *Nimrod* to contend with, Orleans had the *H.M.S. Newcastle*. Admiral Lord Howe demanded that Orleans pay $1,000 or else he would order the destruction of the town's saltworks. Neighboring Eastham coughed up $1,200 to save their saltworks; Brewster paid the Brits $4,000. Orleans decided they were not going to pay the ransom and told the British to just try and collect. Thus began the Battle of Rock Harbor.

The *Newcastle* was a large vessel and could not get close enough to the Orleans coast to do any major damage. She lobbed her cannonballs toward the mainland only to see them land harmlessly in the marshes. Moving closer to shore, she ran aground. Yet this did not stop the British. They burned two sloops in the harbor, the *Washington* and the *Nancy*, and seized two other vessels, the schooner *Betsy* and the sloop *Camel*. A local sailor was made pilot of the *Betsy* and was ordered to sail the vessel to Boston. He, of course, had other ideas and swiftly ran the *Betsy* aground off Yarmouth where Cape Codders then recaptured her. The *Camel* was never reclaimed by the Yankees.

Back at Rock Harbor the Orleans militia successfully repelled the Brits' attempted landing, killing a number of the invaders in the process. Sixty years after the battle, the living survivors of the militia, or their surviving widows, received one hundred and sixty acres of land as a token of thanks.

Another British vessel harassing the Cape coastline and blockading Cape ports was the *H.M.S. Spenser*. Commodore Richard Ragget was demanding ransoms from each town to save their saltworks. Attempting to run the blockade in a whaleboat full of provisions were two deep water ship masters, Captain Matthew Hopheny "Hoppy" Mayo and Captain Winslow L. Knowles. The crew of the *Spenser* captured them and Hoppy Mayo was forced to act as pilot of a Yankee vessel that was seized by the British. His orders were to navigate the ship up the coast to Wellfleet. Mayo complied, but he had a plan.

Aided by a patch of stormy weather, Mayo set his plan in motion.

Claiming that the storm and the shoals made continuing any further a dangerous proposition, he convinced the British to anchor the vessel off Eastham. He then managed to get the entire crew of twenty-three below decks with enough rum to get them all fairly drunk. Up top by himself, Mayo rounded up all the weapons he could find and tossed them overboard, except for two brass pistols, which he put in his jacket. He then cut the anchor line and allowed the ship to drift with the storm until it ran aground at low tide.

The crew finally emerged on deck to find Mayo with pistols drawn. He calmly climbed over the side of the vessel and walked across the flats to land where he mustered a group of Eastham men who followed him out to the grounded vessel and took the entire British crew captive. They were then marched to Tom Crosby's Tavern where the Yanks and Brits raised pints together. The prisoners were later taken to a barn where they spent the remainder of the night. The next morning the whole lot escaped and stole back the Yankee vessel!

Mad Jack & Molasses

Perhaps Barnstable's most famous and most flamboyant sea captain was none other than Captain John Percival, known locally as "Mad Jack" Percival or simply "Roaring Jack." Much of his fame may come from legends that over the years galvanized into assumed truths.

He went to sea at a very early age and lived a good long life, to age eighty-three. The events that took place between those years are largely speculation. One popular legend involves him leaving home at age thirteen after an argument with his parents over hasty pudding. Another tale not only places Percival at the Battle of Trafalgar on October 21, 1805 as Lord Nelson's British fleet defeated a combined French and Spanish armada during the Napoleonic Wars, but places him in the middle of the conflict as commander of Nelson's flagship, *Victory* !

By the War of 1812, Percival achieved the rank of captain, and his exploits would earn him the nickname of "Mad Jack." At New York Harbor on July 4, 1813, in a fishing boat with a crew of thirty-

two he surprised and subsequently captured the British vessel
Beagle, simply his way of celebrating Independence Day. There
would be other prizes during the war and other tales of his voyages to the West Indies. His 1825 voyage to Hawaii as commander
of the schooner *Dolphin*, the first such visit to the islands by a
United States warship, resulted in riots and years of unrest.

But Captain Percival will forever be remembered for the years
from 1841 to 1846 during which time he was associated with *USS
Constitution*. In fact, Percival is credited with saving *"Old Ironsides"*
from being scrapped when the Navy Department deemed her
beyond repair. According to the Navy, repairs would cost $150,000,
a fortune in those days. Percival scoffed at the Navy's claim and
price tag, and promised that he could oversee the repairs for a
mere $10,000. Percival was true to his word, and when the repairs
were concluded for the specified $10,000 the Navy placed "Mad
Jack," then sixty-five years of age, in command with orders to sail
the grand warship around the world. The voyage lasted for nearly
five hundred days, covering more than 50,000 miles and forever
established the vessel and the man as U.S. Navy institutions.

Meanwhile, the Lower Cape town of Orleans had its own war
hero. Born at the height of the Revolutionary War, Joshua Crosby
went to sea at the young age of thirteen on board a fishing boat. He
later sailed on whaling vessels and coastal schooners, but would
forever be remembered for his service on board the warship *USS
Constitution*.

Earlier trained on whalers as a gunner battling pirates off the
Barbary Coast, this experience served him well when he became a
quarterdeck gunnery officer on the *Constitution*. His most memorable battle took place on August 19, 1812 when *"Old Ironsides"*
engaged the British warship *HMS Guerriere* off the coast of Massachusetts. This encounter resulted in a Yankee victory, the first
major American victory of the war. Crosby and his crew were
credited with delivering a key assault against the *Guerriere* that
helped to bring about the victory. Crosby trained his gun on the
mizzenmast, bringing it down and causing the Brits to surrender
less than thirty minutes later.

There is an interesting side story to this battle that concerns a barrel of molasses on board the *Guerriere's* deck, which may have contributed to the victory. Molasses was used to concoct a "land-lubbers" drink called switchel. For a seafarer to be offered this landlubber drink was considered an insult of the highest order. In anticipation of a British victory, the *Guerriere's* crew rolled a barrel of molasses up top in plain view of the Americans — the nine-teenth century's nautical way of "thumbing your nose" at the opposition. Yet, the move backfired on the Brits. The *Constitution's* gunners destroyed the barrel, spilling slippery molasses all about the *Guerriere's* deck, thus making it nearly impossible for the British to keep their footing and maneuver their vessel.

With the *Constitution* being overhauled in 1813, Crosby partici-pated in the Battle of Lake Erie on September 10 of that year, another American victory. He rejoined the *Constitution* in 1814 to help capture two more British warships before the war's conclu-sion. Crosby remained at sea for the next quarter century moving cargoes along the East Coast and across the Atlantic. Retiring from the sea at age sixty, he became keeper of the Three Sisters Light-houses at Nauset for the next sixteen years. In his mid-seventies he became a farmer for the remaining years of his life, which ended in December 1861 at the age of eighty-two.

The Woman Who Saved Hyannis

There is a tale of a woman who outsmarted a troop of British soldiers during the War of 1812, and by doing so saved the village of Hyannis.

At that time during the war, Hyannis was an important Cape port. Unfortunately, defending it against enemy invasion was a difficult task. When the news went out that the British were bearing down on Hyannis with plans to capture the port and pillage the village, her residents decided to flee rather than face the oncoming attack. There were no troops to put forth a defense. The only option, it seemed, was to escape.

Yet one Hyannis resident, a woman, decided that she would not leave her home. She would face the British, alone, but not without a strategy.

Very soon all the other buildings were vacant, save one.

That night the British arrived. The woman did not even bother to douse her light. Since all else was dark, the troops approached this solitary lit dwelling to find the woman alone in an otherwise deserted village.

They asked her what happened to the villagers. She replied that they departed earlier that day.

They asked her why she alone stayed behind. Her answer was that she stayed behind to care for her husband.

And what is the problem with your husband? they asked.

"He has smallpox," she replied, "there has been an outbreak in the village and many have died."

Fearful of contracting the disease, the British troops quickly departed and sent out the order for other British vessels to avoid the port of Hyannis. The village was spared and the population returned to their homes, thanks to the heroic actions of a quick thinking woman.

Cape Cod and the Civil War

When the Civil War came in the middle of the last century, Cape Codders were already struggling with the great questions of the day relating to national unity and slavery. Despite the rural and semi-isolated nature of the Cape, inhabitants were not unaware of the growing regional tensions that created two separate societies in the nation.

The coasting trade, dominated by New England vessels, connected the economies of the north and south and sailing crews brought back first hand knowledge of how the country was evolving into two very different camps. Cape Codders in the nineteenth century were surprisingly literate and were kept abreast of national events by a wide arrangement of newspapers and pamphlets.

As to the institution of slavery, it existed on a small scale in New England up through the eighteenth century. The economy, which was fully centered on free-labor and industry, ruled out the widespread use of slaves although there are plenty of local records that show Cape Codders owned their share of personal "servants"

Civil War Monument at Orleans. (J. Sheedy photo)

as late as the first years of the nineteenth century. There was an ambivalence on the part of most Cape Codders when it came to placing moral judgements on those who endorsed the "peculiar institution." Since it was the law of the land, the majority was generally content to leave slavery where it existed.

Some churches split over the contradiction of slavery and the message of Christianity, but there was never a strong local abolitionist sentiment. Indeed, some of the worst riots over the slavery question happened on the Cape in the 1840s when abolitionists attempted to hold rallies in Harwich. They were beaten and run out of town by citizens who felt that it was an issue for southerners to decide. Certainly there were committed abolitionists, like

Captain Jonathan Walker of Harwich, who risked their lives to bring escaped slaves north to freedom, and there was a small but well organized chapter of the Underground Railroad on the Cape. But these individuals and organizations were exceptions and the issue of slavery incited little fervor.

On the second, and larger issue of Union, there was, however, no ambivalence. When the first rebel shots were fired on Fort Sumter in the spring of 1861, there was a swell of enthusiasm for God, Father Abraham, and Union. Each Cape Cod town was quickly able to fill the initial quota for troops. Captain Charles Chipman led a contingent of "three months men," called the "Sandwich Guards," to Boston where they were immediately moved south to be in place to defend Washington DC. Large amounts of money were pledged by each town in spring town meetings for the support of what was expected to be a short and glorious expedition.

Cape Cod might have been expected to make its major contribution in providing enlistments for the navy. In fact, volunteers seemed to be generally split between the army and the navy. In both services, hundreds of volunteers passed the four years of the conflict with a combination of long periods of boredom and loneliness coupled with short, intense moments of terror and blood. Beginning with Bull Run in the early days of the war, to the final surrender of Lee's army at Appomatox Courthouse in Virginia, Cape men were involved in all of the major campaigns.

Some men were wounded and ended their war service as invalids. Others suffered multiple wounds and continued to serve in the line for the duration of the war. John Ryder of Brewster saw action from 1862 until being wounded at Kenesaw Mountain in 1864. He survived the conflict and lived until 1929. Captain Chipman, who led the first contingent from the county, reached the rank of Lt. Colonel and died of wounds suffered in the siege of Petersburg in August of 1864.

Others, like Henry Knippe of Sandwich, Solomon Doane and Jonathan Gifford of Harwich, Benjamin Lombard of Truro, and Zabina Dill of Chatham, died in the infamous Andersonville, South Carolina Confederate prison. Cold Harbor, Fredericksburg, Chancellorsville, Petersburg, and Vicksburg were just some of the battlefields that claimed the lives of Cape Codders. In all, almost three thousand men served in the Union forces during the Civil War. This was almost ten percent of the population of the Cape at that time.

The exposed geography of Cape Cod posed a possible danger from Confederate privateers throughout the war years. Ship captains, such as Benjamin Howes of Dennis who saw his beautiful clipper *Southern Cross* captured and burned by the raider *Florida*, and Eastham's Captain Edward Penniman, who barely escaped having his New Bedford whaler *Minerva* sunk by the *Shenandoah*, were living testimony to the possibility of a rebel attack from the sea. Captain Franklin Percival lost his ship *Charles Hill* to the Confederate privateer *Alabama* while sailing off the coast of South America.

Concerned about its vulnerability, Provincetown prevailed on the national government to build two forts on Long Point. These structures were later named "Fort Useless" and "Fort Harmless" as the threat of rebel invasion failed to materialize. Benjamin F. Robbins of Harwich noted in his journal that a Confederate raid on Cape Cod was unlikely, but he did cite an instance where a stranded steamer fired some cannons in Nantucket Sound, putting the town in a panic.

A few individuals rose to prominence during the war as a result of their exploits. Ezra C. Baker of Barnstable was given a field commission for bravery at Cold Harbor when he risked his life to bring his dead commander off the battlefield. Prentice H. Davis, also of Barnstable, served with the 24th Massachusetts Regiment and was decorated for gallant conduct at Morris Island. Sergeant Richard Lombard of Truro saw action in twenty-seven battles and skirmishes and was officially cited twice for bravery.

Joseph E. Hamblin, who was born in Yarmouth, was given a battlefield promotion to Brevet Brigadier General on the recommendation of General Phil Sheridan, after valorous service in the major battles of Antietam, Fredericksburg, and Chancellorsville. Hamblin became the highest-ranking Cape Codder in the Union army. He was on active duty for the duration of the war, save for a few months while recovering from wounds suffered at Cedar Creek. But the vast majority of soldiers and sailors served their enlistments in obscurity, grateful that they were able to survive the appalling slaughter that marked the conflict.

The Civil War had effects on the economy and society of Cape Cod that lasted far beyond the conflict. Fisheries were very much reduced during the war, as were the traditional markets that supported maritime enterprise along the Atlantic coast. The merchant marine never returned to its prominence. A strong prewar whaling industry also went into a decline. Subsequent postwar economic woes, which continued into the twentieth century, saw a slow but steady reduction in the population of the peninsula as young people moved away for better opportunities.

The experience of the war was never forgotten. Books were written and memorials constructed to commemorate the great national fratricide that came to be known in the North as the War of the Rebellion. Long after the struggle ended, veterans of the Grand Army of the Republic mustered annually in parades and reunions. It was at these gatherings that old warriors exchanged stories about lost youth and the war that changed the destiny of the nation.

Germany's Attack on Orleans

At 1 a.m. on Sunday, July 21, 1918, the nearly one hundred and forty-foot long tug *Perth Amboy* chugged into Gloucester Harbor with two coal barges in tow. At Gloucester she picked up another barge, *No. 740*, and then left Gloucester on a southerly track to pick up a fourth barge. Their route would be taking them along the backside of the Cape, and a rendezvous with history.

Master of the *Perth Amboy* was Captain Joe Tapley. Along for the trip was Tapley's wife. In tow, besides barge *No. 740*, were *No. 703*, *No. 766* and the barge *Lansford*. All four barges were more than one hundred and fifty feet long, with the largest being about one hundred and ninety feet.

Daybreak found the five vessels off the Highland cliffs near the tip of the Cape and by 10:30 a.m. they were about three miles off Orleans and about ten miles from the Orleans Coast Guard Station. As was typical for a July morning there was a slight fog upon the water. On board the barges were many family members of the captains and crews enjoying a leisurely cruise on a peaceful Sunday morning. Of the thirty or so people on board the five vessels, about a quarter were women and children.

On board the *Lansford* were Captain Charles Ainsleigh and his wife and young boy. Meanwhile, across the water on *No. 740* were Captain Joe Perry and his wife and daughter. His sole crewman also brought along his family. The women of *No. 740* were preparing breakfast when the calm Sunday morning erupted with a sudden explosion.

All eyes on the tug and barges scanned the eastern horizon to find that a German U-boat had surfaced and was firing upon the defenseless armada. The submarine was more than two hundred feet long and was armed with two deck guns. The wooden barges didn't stand a chance against the barrage of nearly one hundred and fifty shells fired upon them. The crews quickly abandoned ship and watched as three of the barges, *No. 703*, *No. 740* and *No. 766*, disappeared beneath the waves. *Lansford* lasted a bit longer; sinking on the following day. Captain Ainsleigh of that barge suffered injuries to both his arms when a shell exploded onboard his vessel. His young boy, it has been told, grabbed his father's rifle and fired upon the German sub. It is also said that the boy saved the American flag when the crew abandoned ship.

On shore, hundreds of people lined the beaches to watch the events transpiring off shore. Churches opened their doors early when news of the attack was learned. All agreed that the Germans were rather poor shots as it took so many shells to sink the four vessels. The *Perth Amboy*, which had a steel hull, survived the attack though her deck was riddled with holes and she was left burning, her crew leaving the vessel in lifeboats.

Meanwhile, two rescue efforts were underway - one by land and one by sea. The newly completed Chatham air base was only ten miles away, but unfortunately, a good many of the boys were at a baseball game in Provincetown that morning. Eventually, one plane went up to repel the invaders, though some reports claim that three planes were sent. The Chatham aviators dropped either dud bombs or else tools, notably, a monkey wrench, at the escaping U-boat. Very soon the German vessel submerged and the US plane returned to its base.

During the course of the one-sided battle, Captain Robert Pierce of the Chatham Coast Guard Station telephoned up to Provincetown to speak with his supervisor. Pierce was a bit unsure about what to do in a situation such as this. He knew he should launch a surfboat to save the survivors of the sinking vessels, but at the same time he was not sure if he could order his men to enter a battle in progress. The word came down from Provincetown to launch his boat and land the survivors.

By the time Pierce and his crew arrived at the scene one of the barges had already been sunk. All the crews were in lifeboats. The U-boat was still firing upon the *Perth Amboy* and the three remaining barges. They were also firing at the beach, and possibly even at the lifeboats and Coast Guard surfboat. Pierce assessed the situation and decided that the injured, *Lansford* Captain Ainsleigh and a *Perth Amboy* crewman with a wound on his arm, needed to be brought ashore right away. He took the injured personnel on board his surfboat and headed toward the beach, urging the others in the lifeboats to follow after him. All involved were safely landed.

Though there were hundreds of witnesses to the events of that morning, the accounts differ greatly. Some reports state the whole ordeal lasted a half-hour while other reports cite an hour and a half as the duration. Some accounts say that one shell hit the beach, making Orleans the only place in the United States to be attacked during World War I, while other accounts state that a number of rounds hit the beach and some hit the marsh beyond.

The German U-boat, it is said, fired about one hundred and fifty shells although some reports give a figure of less than one hundred. And we may never know how many planes were sent up from Chatham air station, whether one, two or three, and whether they dropped bombs or a monkey wrench.

The wounded were taken up to Boston, their crews and families joining them on the following day. The *Perth Amboy* was later towed to New York for repairs.

And the waters off Orleans tumbled once again with waves and whitecaps, erasing all evidence of the events that marked July 21, 1918 as the first attack in American waters since the War of 1812.

Chapter
7

Nearly Forgotten Places & Faces

Cape Cod is a trove of well-known locations and sites dotting its landscape, locations and sites that set this peninsula apart as something truly unique and that help to define its very spirit.

Yet, for every familiar landmark, there are many other historical locations ... some with us still, some long since gone ... that each played their part in making Cape Cod what it was way back then, and what it is today.

Some of those nearly forgotten places, and the nearly forgotten faces associated with them, are remembered in this section. A canal in Orleans, a Boston railway tower now residing above the cliffs of Truro, a wireless station in Wellfleet, and an Eastham cottage washed away by the great Blizzard of 1978 all help to define that truly special Cape Cod spirit.

Cape Cod's Other Canal

The Cape Cod Canal is certainly one of the most memorable geographic features of this area. It is an engineering marvel stretching from Buzzards Bay to Cape Cod Bay. The impressive waterway cuts through an almost eight mile swath of land to create a navigable channel that has been of great benefit to mariners passing along the Atlantic coast. Some Cape Codders will even tell you that you really are not on Cape Cod until you cross over it.

What is not so well-known is that the Cape Cod Canal is not the first man-made waterway to be built on the peninsula. In fact, almost two hundred years before the present canal was opened in 1914, another canal was serving the needs of Cape Cod sailors. This small and now forgotten waterway was located at the border of Orleans and Eastham and was called by some historians "Jeremiah's Drain." Those who live on the outer Cape know the old ditch as "Jeremiah's Gutter."

Geological evidence points to the fact that for centuries salt water flow was common through the marshy area that begins at Boat Meadow Creek on the Orleans bay side and moves eastward toward Town Cove and Nauset Harbor. This was especially true at seasonal high course tides. There is even some evidence that one of Cape Cod's early explorers, Bartholomew Gosnold, may have been fooled when he saw the flooded waterway and it led him to the false observation that the outer Cape was an island.

As populations grew on Cape Cod in the seventeenth and eighteenth centuries, south side sailors found the distance around the tip of Provincetown to the bay side ports to be both lengthy and dangerous, particularly in the area of the shoals of Peaked Hill Bars off Truro. The solution was to deepen the natural cut, which became Jeremiah's Gutter.

In the spring of 1717, the channel was opened across the land of Jeremiah Smith, connecting Boat Meadow Creek on the bay to Town Cove. From this protected harbor, boats could reach the Atlantic through Nauset Harbor. Never very wide and subject to the problems of low tides and bayside sand bars, the channel nevertheless accommodated small boats of up to twenty tons and cut the time of shipping around the Lower Cape by as much as a full day.

In the same year that it was opened, the canal played a role in the wreck of the pirate ship *Whidah* when His Majesty's agent, Captain Cyprian Southack, used it to take a survey party to the wreck site. After arriving by boat from Boston, Southack obtained a whaleboat in Provincetown and proceeded down the bay and through Jeremiah's Gutter to the Atlantic side where the *Whidah* went aground on the Wellfleet shore in an early spring storm. Although his trip through the canal was smooth enough, his mission of preserving the treasure from the site for the crown was not so successful because he found that enterprising residents already made off with most of the valuables.

When the south precinct of Eastham was established as the town of Orleans in 1797, the Smith family land and Jeremiah's Gutter became the northern boundary of the new town. In 1804 the canal was improved and widened.

Jeremiah's Gutter was important during the War of 1812 when British warships *Newcastle* and *Spenser* blockaded Cape Cod Bay. The larger British vessels were unable to sail close in to the shore because of the shoals. Local sailors used smaller shallow draft whaleboats to move cargo through the narrow canal from the bay to the Atlantic. Use of the canal prevented seizure of valuable supplies that were badly needed while the war was in progress.

The nineteenth century saw a gradual decline in the use of Jeremiah's Gutter. There was some post-war interest in widening the small canal and around 1820 a company called the Eastham and Orleans Canal Proprietors was actually formed "for purpose of opening, and keeping open a canal from Norset Cove {sic} to Boat Meadow Creek." The proposal planned to charge a ten cent a ton toll for vessels passing through the waterway, with additional charges for certain kinds of cargo. But nothing was ever done and after three years the charter for the company lapsed. Certainly part of the problem was that a larger canal in the Orleans area would still not have eliminated the navigation problems of the Monomoy Shoals off Chatham and the dangerous Peaked Hill Bars. The use of larger vessels and the problems of wide tidal flats in Cape Cod Bay also made such a passage in the Orleans-Eastham area impractical.

Today, there is little evidence of Cape Cod's first canal. Those who frequent the shopping complex near the Eastham rotary at Route 6 are usually unaware that they are walking on the site of Jeremiah's Gutter. Canal Road in Orleans is the only visible remembrance that the small waterway ever existed.

Forgotten Sailors – Seafaring Women of Cape Cod

The maritime past of Cape Cod recalls the stories of captains who drove their ships and men across vast stretches of ocean in the pursuit of fortunes and adventure. Libraries are filled with the exploits of these "Blue Water Men" and their impact on history.

Indeed, it is difficult to pass through a Cape Cod village without some reference to an important local shipmaster who put the place on the map. What is perhaps less known is that many women from Cape Cod went to sea along with their men. The adventures and experiences of these women are not generally found in the history books. The neglected history of women at sea is a rich and necessary part of the nautical lore that connects Cape Cod and the sea.

Only recently have historians begun to examine the seagoing journals kept by women and these materials are adding another dimension to the picture of what life was like aboard ships in the last century.

A century or more ago, as American trading and whaling interests took ships and crews to the far corners of the earth, it became increasingly common for the wives of sea captains to accompany their husbands to foreign ports.

Along with their husbands, these women experienced seasickness, mutinies, pirate attacks, storms and shipwrecks. Often making their first voyages as newly married young women, the wives of shipmasters entered a male-dominated culture where the presence of a female on a ship was often considered bad luck by many crewmembers.

They lived in a pyramid shaped social structure where the

Mrs. Jerusha Sturgis Howes of Dennis accompanied her husband, Captain Moses Howes, on a number of clipper ship voyages. (J. Coogan Collection)

captain took the top position followed by the descending hierarchy of mates and seamen. The position of the captain's wife was a tenuous and delicate one. Naturally near the top of the pyramid with her husband, she still had to be careful so as not to appear to eclipse his authority. Women who appeared to wield undue influence aboard a vessel could earn the ship the dubious title "hen frigate" from a superstitious crew.

Relations were always delicate between the wives and the men who operated the ship. She could not appear too close or yet become too distant to the ship's routine, lest the men begin to focus their own loneliness or frustrations on her. Often she was socially isolated and without the association of other females for long periods of time. Sailors could be particularly cruel if they took a dislike to the captain's wife.

"She is the meanest, most hoggish and the greediest female that has ever existed," one sailor wrote in reference to his captain's wife. "Her looks is dispised by everyone on board and the whistle of a gale of wind through the rigging is much more musical than the sound of her voice."[1]

For the woman who might have to serve as a surgeon, cook, and surrogate mother to young and undisciplined crewmembers it could be a lonely and often frustrating experience.

One wife commented on her ship's first mate, noting, "Without exception I think him nearest to a savage of anyone I have ever met. He possesses a very quick, ungovernable temper, is also very jealous and is very ignorant of the rules of good breeding. And yet he has a high opinion of himself!"[2]

The captain and his wife, often accompanied by their children, lived in the aft cabin at the stern of the ship. The crew was billeted in the forecastle up forward and it was not expected that the men would enter the family quarters. The rules were described by one woman who wrote "A strict code of etiquette is maintained aboard these ships. The second and third mates and carpenter are served at our table after we are through. The steward eats in the pantry; the cook in his galley. The men of the crew, and the boys, have their meals, in fine weather, on the forward part of the deck. Where there is a storm, they are served in their own quarters."[3]

The nineteenth century sea journals of women are filled with remarks about constant seasickness, comments about strange and exotic foreign cultures, and references to the dangers of heavy weather. Forecasts were non-existent and vessels often found themselves in the teeth of tremendous gales. Mary Mathews Bray of Yarmouth, who was with her father aboard the ship *National Eagle*, described one stormy experience, noting, "It is difficult to write. I have to grasp my paper with one hand, my pen with the other, and brace my knees against the table, lest we all part company."[4]

Georgianna Dyer, who sailed from Provincetown aboard the whaling schooner *Ellen A. Swift* with her husband Captain J. Emmons Dyer, found herself in a storm off the Hatteras whaling grounds. Her ship was so battered that she later compared the experience of being thrown around the cabin to that of being like a bowling ball.

Sally Mayo Lavender, also from Provincetown, recounted her experience of trying to sleep in a March Atlantic storm aboard the brig *Panama*. "I clung to the sides (of the berth) to prevent being thrown out and for a moment I am lost. I hardly know whether I am in the berth or on the floor."[5]

In the Far East trade there was the particular danger of pirates. In 1865, off the coast of China, Mrs. Lucy Lord Howes of Dennis, who was aboard the small clipper *Lubra*, saw her husband, Captain Benjamin P. Howes, murdered by pirates in their cabin. Left for dead by the departing pirates who set the ship on fire, she was able, with the help of several surviving crewmen, to douse the flames and make repairs to the damaged ship, working it back to one of the Chinese treaty ports and safety.

During this experience, Mrs. Howes had her two children with her, both of whom were under the age of four.

Besides the constant seasickness, there was always the possibility that a ship might founder and sink in stormy seas. Mary Connolly of Dennis was with her husband aboard the ship *South America* when it struck an uncharted reef off the coast of West Africa. As the ship took on water and began to break up, Mrs. Connolly was lashed to pieces of wreckage and with the survivors, floated to the barren and isolated coast. For several weeks before being rescued she experienced near starvation and the threat of hostile natives.

Diadama Kelley Doane of West Harwich survived the 1877 sinking of her husband's clipper ship *Granger* off the coast of Borneo by riding in an open whaleboat for almost a week before being picked up by a passing ship.

Women who visited foreign ports were exposed to cultures that

those who remained at home could hardly imagine. From the foot
binding practices of China to exotic foods and unusual birds, Cape
women brought back memories of fascinating foreign adventures
while aboard ship. Young Alice Baxter of South Dennis recalled
seeing the effects of the 1883 explosion of the volcano Krakatoa on
a voyage out to China aboard the ship *Obed Baxter.*

In Shanghai, she experienced travel in the numerous rickshaws
in that city, later recalling, "It cost us two cents a ride in those days
and somehow we felt it was a bigger barrel's worth than the
merry-go-round back home."[6] For Emily Crosby Lincoln of Brewster, it was the embarrassing sight of half-clothed natives that
caught her attention while in Cocanada, India in 1864.

In recounting the tales of seafaring women, it would seem
reasonable to assume that they were the "liberated women" of the
nineteenth century. But this assessment would not be accurate. The
motives of women who went to sea with their husbands were
anything but radical. Rather than an opportunity for breaking new
social ground, most women accepted their role at sea as being both
expected and necessary. They saw the experience as part of preserving a traditional marriage and they acted as supportive
helpmates and partners to their husbands.

But the sight of American ships headed for home from foreign
ports would often induce pangs of loneliness for the comfort of
land-bound extended families far away. Sally Mayo Lavender
summed up the mixed feelings of most seagoing women when she
wrote in her journal, "I felt rather a tinge of homesickness tonight.
But homesickness I could not call it for this is all the home I know at
present; for here are my all: husband and child; but felt isolated."[7]

In much the same vein, Sandwich's Hannah Burgess wrote,
"Once in no other place than my native town could I be happy. No
other friends could please me but my parents and relatives. Now
where my husband is, there is my home. May it ever be thus."[8]

Ruth of Wakeby Lake

Up in the highlands of South Sandwich in the old neighborhood
of "Farmersville," is one of Cape Cod's most magnificent stretches

of fresh water. The connected Wakeby and Mashpee lakes lie to the east of Forestdale, bordering Mashpee in a section of town that was originally called "the Plains."

For most of its history, this gentle pond-spotted landscape was a farming community inhabited by generations of Hoxies, Meiggs and Ewers. The lakes became attractive to outsiders in the period following the Civil War as increasing numbers of fishermen discovered the rewards of angling in the clear waters. In this period, a Wampanoag Native American operated a small summer excursion steamboat on the lake that became popular with sightseers and fishermen.

Benjamin Boardley of Mashpee was raised in a town that was created around the heritage of his Native American ancestors. Like most of his contemporaries, there is little evidence that Boardley had any long-term formal schooling. Most inhabitants of the town were subsistence farmers who scratched out an existence in much the same fashion as their native ancestors did for generations. But Benjamin Boardley was a natural genius when it came to engines. He began to design and build steam-powered machines that he eventually adapted to water craft. Since he lived in the vicinity of the Wakeby and Mashpee lakes, he was quick to see that people would pay to be transported to points along the shore.

Boardley contracted with Herbert Crosby of Osterville to build a thirty-five-foot craft for use on the lakes and it went into service in the 1880s. The single-boiler power plant was designed by Boardley and drove two balanced side wheels that were mounted amidships. The original name of the vessel was *Quichatasett*. The small steamboat became a popular attraction for people who visited then rural South Sandwich and was operated for more than thirty years by Boardley and his son, William.

At least on one occasion the *Quichatasett* carried President Grover Cleveland and some of his fishing buddies to their favorite sections of the lakes. Though not documented, it is probably not just coincidental that in the period of the Cleveland presidency, and his frequent fishing excursions to South Sandwich from his summer home at Gray Gables, the name of Boardley's steamer was changed to *Ruth*, most likely for the President's oldest daughter.

Records are sketchy and even Boardley's descendants are not exactly sure why the original name of the vessel was changed. What is known is that the *Ruth* continued to operate on the lakes until the beginning of the second decade of this century and then the trail of the steamer seems to drift into obscurity.

The Jenny Lind Tower

Sitting on a lonely bluff just south of Highland Light in North Truro is the so-called Jenny Lind Tower. Most tourists know nothing about the structure and few Cape Codders have ever visited it.

More than fifty-five feet high, the granite tower looks something like a miniature Provincetown Monument but it was not the inspiration for that structure. Originally part of the Fitchburg Railroad Depot building in Boston, when the depot was razed the tower was purchased and moved to its present location in 1927 by Boston attorney Harry M. Aldrich.

There are two stories as to why the tower came to be where it is. The first is that Mr. Aldrich's grandfather was an official with the Boston and Maine Railroad that originally built the depot. It is thought by some that Mr. Aldrich wanted a suitable memorial for his grandfather and chose to move one of the four turrets to a piece of land that he owned in Truro.

The second and certainly more interesting tale revolves around the personality of Jenny Lind, the nineteenth-century European singer known as the "Swedish Nightingale," and Mr. Aldrich's admiration for her.

In the 1850s, shortly after the tower was built, during an East Coast tour, Ms. Lind reportedly sang from the tower to a Boston crowd. Mr. Aldrich was almost certainly too young to have been personally in attendance at Ms. Lind's performance, but the story is that he was apparently so taken by accounts of the Scandinavian singer's beauty that he carried a life-long torch for her. He read everything about her he could get his hands on and saved any memorabilia that celebrated her career.

When the depot was being torn down in 1927, he brought the

Jenny Lind Tower of the Truro Highlands. (J. Coogan Collection)

tower to the Cape in sections by railroad car and had it rebuilt, stone
by numbered stone, in North Truro as a personal tribute to Ms. Lind.
It took five men more than two months to reassemble the tower.

Whether Mr. Aldrich ever visited his completed monument is
lost to the memory of those who live in Truro today. Few people
make the walk to it anymore. It is now the home of pigeons, owls

and white-tailed deer. The late Tom Kane, who knew as much about Truro history as just about anyone (and who also appreciated a good story), said that on moonlit nights when the wind is just right it is possible to hear the voice of the soprano coming from the direction of the tower.[9]

Orleans and the French Connection

Orleans is only one of two towns in Barnstable County that does not trace the origin of its name to either a place in England, or to a particular Cape Cod person.

Perhaps most unusual is that the town's name is French in a part of New England that has especially strong roots in the British isles. The French influence, in a community that was started by such English families as Crosby, Nickerson, Knowles, Linnell, Newcomb, Sparrow, and Wixon, began with the town's incorporation near the end of the eighteenth century. Founded shortly after the close of the American Revolution in a time when Britain's actions continuously reminded her former colonies that she considered the separation as only temporary, it appears that the local citizenry had no interest in adopting a name that would in any way connect them with their former colonial master.

Some say that the name Orleans was selected in an effort to honor the French-American Revolutionary War alliance. Still others claim that the name reflected local support for the exiled Duke of Orleans who was residing in Boston at the time.

At any rate, the French connection has been a part of the town since it separated from Eastham in 1797. Almost a century after Orleans became a separate town, the French connection literally became true.

As the first transatlantic telegraph cables were laid in the period following the American Civil War, it was natural that Cape Cod would become a land terminus for the communication system.

A French cable first connected Europe to America in 1869. Extending considerably to the east of the American land mass, the Cape was the closest connection to Europe. In 1879 an insulated seven copper wire cable was connected from Eastham to the French island of St. Pierre-Miquelon south of Newfoundland, allowing an indirect telegraph link from Europe to the United States.

The Eastham cable station was housed in a two and a half story building near the Three Sisters Lighthouses. The site was, however, considered remote and difficult to reach in rough weather. In 1890, a new station was built near the center of Orleans on Town Cove and the Eastham site was discontinued. In 1898, a direct cable was laid between Doelen, a suburb of Brest, France and Orleans, bypassing St. Pierre-Miquelon. A second cable laid at the same time went directly from France to New York. For many years the two cables were the quickest method of transmitting information from Europe to the United States.

The great distance across the Atlantic made it impossible to transmit standard Morse code sound. Instead, the electrically transmitted signal was converted at the receiving end to strike a paper tape so that the punched Morse code letters could be read by the operators. A number of French operators came to Orleans from St. Pierre-Miquelon and acted as translators. It has been claimed by some that the large number of mansard or "French roofed houses" in these two towns originated with the arrival of the French cable workers.

While the New York to France cable link was the primary transatlantic message route, the Orleans site saw its share of important events. In November of 1898, the Orleans cable notified the world of the sinking of the Steamer *Portland*.

In 1915, it reported the sinking of the *Lusitania*. During World War I the station served as an important communications link for American commanders. In 1927, the news of Charles A. Lindbergh's successful transatlantic flight was telegraphed through the Orleans station. During some of the major hurricanes of the first part of this century the cable was often the only Cape link to the outside world. During World War II the station was closed as Germany occupied France and it was not re-opened until 1952.

Less important in a changing world of communications technology, the station closed for the final time on November 24, 1959 after signaling Thanksgiving greetings to its listeners.

Since 1971 the Orleans station has been open during the summer months as the French Cable Station Museum. It is located at the corner of Cove Road and Route 28.

Marconi Station

The easternmost edges of Wellfleet greet the realm and majesty of the sea. To the south can be seen the white and then red beams of Nauset Light calling out across the miles. To the north rests a cluster of "outermost" houses, huddled amidst the sand dunes and the sea grass beneath a deep blue morning sky. And between these two horizons is the titanic roar of the ocean, crashing waves spilling the earth's energy upon the sands.

Here in this galaxy of sand and sky and sea is the site of the Marconi wireless station, also known as the South Wellfleet wireless transmitting station. On January 19, 1903 this station sent a message from President Theodore Roosevelt to Edward VII, King of England, making the site the first US transatlantic wireless telegraph station.

The Marconi station and its place in history have been the topic of discussion of late. There has been some debate over whether the Wellfleet station sent the first transatlantic wireless message. Debate can be ended with these simple words: It was not.

The first transatlantic signal, which consisted of the letter "S," was sent from England to Newfoundland in December 1901, the year before the Wellfleet station was completed. During 1902, the first message spanned the Atlantic, sent from England and received at Nova Scotia. Shortly thereafter the Roosevelt to Edward VII message was sent from Wellfleet, making it the first transatlantic message sent from the United States.

This historic message had its beginnings a quarter century earlier with the birth of Italian inventor Guglielmo Marconi. He was born in Bologna on April 25, 1874. By the age of sixteen Marconi was already experimenting at home on wireless modes of telegraphy and was actually successful in sending signals short distances across his parents' back yard. In 1895, at the tender age of twenty-one, he transmitted a signal one mile. Four years later, in 1899, he was successful in sending messages over a span of twenty miles from ship to shore. Next he spanned the English channel, and in 1901, the Atlantic.

Marconi selected a number of sites as transmitting stations, in Newfoundland, Nova Scotia, and at Wellfleet. Construction on the Wellfleet station began in 1901, but a severe storm destroyed the towers and the station had to be rebuilt. Larger towers were erected, four of them each two hundred and ten feet high, to support the antenna network. The towers were constructed of three-inch by twelve-inch lumber and stood on concrete bases. Twelve one-inch steel cables supported each of the towers against the Atlantic winds. The station had a transmitting range of between 1,600 and 3,500 miles.

The transmitter house contained a 20,000 volt condenser, the antenna tuning coil and the whirling sparkgap rotor that could be heard some four miles away. Meanwhile, the power station housed a 45-horsepower generator that supplied 2,200 volts AC, increased to the 20,000 volts necessary to spark the airwaves.

Manning the station were a manager, two engineers and three operators. After the historic 1903 message to Edward VII, the station performed in a commercial capacity. On the evening of April 14/15, 1912, Wellfleet station received a distress call from the sinking White Star liner *Titanic*. That evening, the *Titanic* radio operators were using a new signal of distress, the now familiar SOS, along with the old signal CQD. In fact, it is believed that the *Titanic* was the very first vessel to use the SOS distress call. It is amazing to think that the quiet town of Wellfleet played a role in the greatest ship disaster of all time!

In 1917, as the United States entered the Great War, the Wellfleet station was closed. Three years later, the four massive towers were dismantled and the buildings were abandoned to the elements and the sea. During the Kennedy administration the site was acquired by the National Park Service and made a permanent exhibit.

Atop the cliff are some remains of the original towers and buildings including timbers and sections of the brick footings upon which stood each of the four towers. Cascading down the cliff are the bricks and mortar that once comprised the historic transmitting station. Over the past century the eroding cliff has devoured more than half the land upon which the station once sat.

And today, with imagination, one can believe that above the cliff, two hundred feet in the air, ride the ancient messages that once sparked the Wellfleet skies, ancient messages still audible all these years later: "... SOS ... SOS ... *Titanic* ... sinking fast ... putting women and children off in lifeboats ... cannot last much longer ... come quickly ... SOS ..."

German Gliders at Corn Hill

From the high bluffs that dominate the Outer Cape's ocean threshold, it is a common sight - sea birds wheeling on the air currents that rise from the edge of the beach. Soaring effortlessly, these natural aviators can glide for hours as they search for their next meal.

In the late 1920s human aviators used these same air currents to set gliding records above the Truro and Wellfleet shoreline. The pilots of these motorless aircraft were Germans who were then some of the world leaders in the sport of gliding.

It is probably not coincidental that Germany pioneered motorless flight after World War I. The Treaty of Versailles prohibited Germany from having an air force and restricted the number of pilots that the defeated nation could train and maintain. In an effort to continue the country's progress in aviation in the postwar years, Germany turned to gliding. The famous soaring school at Rossiten produced a number of world-class glider pilots in the mid-1920s.

In 1928, a gliding school was set up on Corn Hill in Truro, financed by J.C. Penny Jr., son of the famous retail store founder. Penny was himself a soaring enthusiast familiar with the Cape's environment. He heard of the German successes in gliding and he wanted to boost the sport in America. Several cottages were rented on the Cape Cod Bay side of Truro just north of Pamet Harbor and a contingent of Germans were invited to bring their equipment and test the air currents there.

Capt. Paul Roehre, the director of the Rossiten school, Paul Laubenthal, an aeronautical engineer, and Peter Hesselbach, one of

Germany's most noted glider pilots, headed up a team of gliding experts who wished to experiment with new machines and techniques in an effort to extend the range of motorless flight.

From all accounts the arrival of the Germans produced a warm, if perhaps curious response from the local farmers and fishermen. The dashing aviators, with their good looks and athletic prowess, most certainly made a very positive impression with the young ladies of Truro and Provincetown. In their frequent excursions around the Lower Cape in a car loaned by Penny, observers noted that they were very well-mannered and polite. Seizing on the local interest in what they were doing, they occasionally enlisted the help of residents in holding the launching lines for their machines as they catapulted from the bluff into the air currents of Cape Cod Bay.

That summer, pilot Hesselbach broke the American record for gliding by staying aloft for more than four hours along his course from Corn Hill to Beach Point. After landing, he estimated that he traveled more than one hundred and twenty miles back and forth across the Truro shoreline. Some people who saw the flight that day said that Hesselbach could have easily stayed up much longer but he landed because he hadn't eaten lunch and was hungry. What was truly remarkable about the flight was the fact that Orville Wright set the previous American record — about ten minutes!

The following summer the gliding school was moved from Corn Hill to South Wellfleet off Le Counts Hollow Road, near Maguire Landing Beach. Cottages were rented from the Cook family and hangers were built to accommodate the machines. Renamed the Cape Cod Gliding School, the enterprise was this time sponsored by the American Motorless Aviation Corp. There were about one hundred and twenty students, including Americans, in the contingent. While the Germans still dominated the sport that summer, one American, Ralph Barnaby, who was on leave from the U.S. Navy, set a record for an American gliding pilot, soaring for more than fifteen minutes before landing near Marconi Beach.

After 1929, there were no more German glider enthusiasts visiting Cape Cod. The worldwide financial crash that took the wind out of the economy also took the air out of the sport of soaring.

Germans and Americans turned inward to confront their own,

more serious challenges. Today there is a monument to these
pioneer glidermen at Corn Hill.

While there is no record to indicate it, one can wonder whether
any of the young Germans who came to Cape Cod to get their first
taste of flying later graduated to the Luftwaffe during World War
II. If so, perhaps for them a bombing run over Plymouth, England
during the Battle of Britain might have brought back momentary
memories of the distant view of Plymouth, Massachusetts a decade
earlier while soaring at the beach off Corn Hill.

Return to the Outermost House

Cable Road in Eastham empties into a land at the outermost
reaches of America where author/naturalist Henry Beston wrote
his classic book *The Outermost House*.

Beyond the red and white column of Nauset Light rests the
beach, the Great Beach, the beach where Henry Beston spent a year
in his small house on a dune to experience life in its simplest and
yet most majestic form.

Here at Nauset Light Beach one can see three generations of
lighthouses, each generation forming a crucial chapter in its
history. Along Cable Road rest the wooden Three Sisters lighthouses that stood on the Eastham cliff during the first two decades
of this century. At the top of the cliff stands the current Nauset
Light where it has cast its beam throughout the past eight decades.
And below, on the beach, lie the jumbled brick remains of the
original lighthouses built in 1837 and that crumbled with the
eroding cliff in 1892, their graves emerging now and then when
violent winter tides excavate the tons and tons of Nauset sand.

A mile south of this spot is the Nauset Coast Guard Station
where can be found a weathered National Seashore placard telling
of Henry Beston's outermost house, which at one time stood yet
another mile or two further south along the Nauset spit. The beach
in this area is worn away, the waves crashing with powerful
purpose, the sands haunted by shipwrecked sailors, surfmen,
beachcombers ... and writers.

It was here, at this seashore universe, where Henry Beston built

*During his solitary year at the "outermost" house, author/naturalist Henry
Beston found comfort and companionship in seeing the beam from Nauset
Lighthouse. (J. Sheedy photo)*

his famed house upon fifty acres of Eastham dune. Beston arrived
at his cottage in the late summer of 1926. His solitary experiment
would put him in touch with the sounds and sights and sensations
of life that we disregard as the backdrop to what we consider more
important things. Beston discovered that the real importance rests
in the wonder of the things we take for granted: the color of beach
sand, the sounds and rhythms of the sea, the migration of birds,
the trek of stars throughout the four seasons, and the ebb and flow
of life itself.

The purpose of his project was simply to celebrate Nature in all its raw glory. At first he did not consider writing a book about his year on the Eastham dune, but within a year after leaving the beach with his pages of notes *The Outermost House* was published. Eight decades later it is considered a classic among books on American nature.

Beston's outermost house on Nauset spit stood as a testament to mankind's reattachment to the world around him. And even though it was swept away by the great Blizzard of 1978 to become part of the majestic landscape, it is still revered by those who connect with the poetic passages of Mr. Beston's classic book. Not just a literary landmark, this stretch of sand where the house once stood is a birthplace of sorts, a place where a man discovered his place in the universe.

Henry Beston was born Henry Beston Sheahan on June 1, 1888 at Quincy, Massachusetts. His father was Irish and his mother, French. Beston, which he took as his pen name and later as his legal name, was his paternal grandmother's family name.

A 1911 graduate of Harvard University, he served in the ambulance corps of the French army and in the US submarine service during the First World War. After the war he stayed on in France for a while to teach at the University of Lyon; Beston was fluent in French. Returning to America, he published five books between 1919 and 1925 before spending his year on the Eastham dune.

After publishing *The Outermost House* in 1928, he married Elizabeth Coatsworth (1893-1986), an author-poet, in 1929. They lived at Hingham, Massachusetts until 1932 when they moved to Nobleboro, Maine to raise their two daughters. Beston continued to write and lecture for the next twenty years, publishing *Chimney Farm Stories* in 1938, *The St. Lawrence* in 1942, *Northern Farm* in 1948 and *White Pines and Blue Water* in 1950.

In 1964 he was honored by the US Department of the Interior for the role he played toward the founding of the Cape Cod National Seashore. On October 11th of that year a ceremony was held on the Eastham beach and the outermost house was dedicated as a literary landmark. A plaque was placed on the house that read: *"The Outermost House in which Henry Beston, author-naturalist, wrote his classic book by that name wherein he sought the great truth and found it in the nature of man."*

Not quite four years later, on April 15, 1968, at the age of seventy-nine, Beston died at Nobleboro, Maine.

The outermost house itself was built in 1926, the plans drawn up during the summer of 1925. Overall, it was twenty feet by sixteen feet, containing two rooms: a main room consisting of a kitchen and sitting area, and a small bedroom. As small as it was, the house had ten windows, the main room with seven and the bedroom with three.

Beston called his place the Fo'castle, short for forecastle, which is the foremast crews' quarters on a ship. It was an appropriate name given the fact that the east facing windows looked out over the sea. On stormy nights, with the waves pounding upon the beach below, it must have felt as if he was at sea riding out a gale.

In the two years before the building of the house, during 1924 and 1925, Beston spent much time on the Lower Cape. He stayed at various inns, at the homes of friends, and even at Highland Light. There is thought that even during the year he lived out on the Eastham dune he spent some of that time inland with friends although his book gives the impression that he spent 365 uninterrupted nights at the house from late summer of 1926 to late summer of 1927.

Over the years following his memorable year on the beach, Beston and his wife would visit the outermost house from time to time. During those years the world outside the little dwelling changed radically. Beston wrote his book during the great prosperity of the Coolidge years. The same year Beston was pondering the life cycle outside his Fo'castle, Lindbergh was flying across the Atlantic. In the couple of years that followed came the Great Depression. Ten years later, Hitler's German war machine was racing across Europe. The world outside the little house would never be the same.

By 1944, as the war in Europe was coming to a close, Beston relocated his house to protect it from tumbling down the eroding dune and into the sea. Also that same year, Beston had a wood stove installed to replace the fireplace.

As Beston became older his visits to Eastham became less frequent. He spent most of his time with his wife at their Chimney Farm in Nobleboro, Maine, publishing very little during the 1950s and 1960s. By 1959, at the age of seventy-one, he presented the Eastham property to the Massachusetts Audubon Society. In that way, other naturalists could visit the dunes and explore the avian populations Beston documented in his book.

The house was used in that capacity for nearly twenty years. Though it faced the hurricanes of 1938 and 1944, which each brought such destruction to the Cape, the Blizzard of 1978 proved to be too powerful. Considered by many to be the hundred year storm of the twentieth century, the winter storm of February 1978 brought unusually high and violent tides sweeping across the Nauset dunes. The house was lifted off its foundation and pushed into Nauset inlet where it floated for a time. But as it drifted out of the protection of the inlet the pounding surf destroyed the house, and devastated the surrounding dune universe, forever altering the land and the flow of the tides in this area.

The better part of a century has passed since Beston's year on the Nauset dune. Turn back the clock and there stands a man along the shoreline taking note of the sound of the waves, the smell of the air, the texture of the sand, the calling of an unseen bird over yonder dune. He listens to the earth's voice, understanding the inner meaning to all that is around us.

Presidential Visits to the Cape

There are very few people who are unaware of the connection of President John F. Kennedy and Cape Cod. The years of the Hyannisport summer White House during the early 1960s did much to bring attention to this area.

More recently, President Clinton's choice of a summer vacation on nearby Martha's Vineyard and Vice President Al Gore's 1996 vacation in Truro again placed an emphasis on this region as a prime summer resort. But while Kennedy's stay on Cape Cod and Clinton's retreat to the Vineyard may have had the most impact because of the extensive media coverage, there were other less well-known visits made by other chief executives that created at least local interest in their day.

The first sitting President to visit Cape Cod was Ulysses S. Grant. In late August of 1874, President and Mrs. Grant arrived in Hyannis from Nantucket on board the Steamer *River Queen*. After disembarking at the long stone pier that jutted out into Nantucket Sound, the eighteenth President was driven up to the railroad depot on Main Street where he made a short speech. From Hyannis, Grant took the train out to Provincetown where there were a few more speeches along the way in Dennis and Wellfleet. After a final round of handshaking and speeches at the Cape-tip, Grant continued on to Boston by steamboat. Grant's visit lasted only a single day.

The first Cape Cod summer White House was not the Kennedy compound in Hyannisport. This honor belongs to the town of Bourne and President Grover Cleveland's summer home at Gray Gables. After serving a single term as President, Cleveland found himself out of office in 1889. He was familiar with Cape Cod from a number of fishing and hunting expeditions that he took to this area while Governor of New York. In 1890 he purchased seven acres of land and a home on the Monument River. When he was re-elected to the presidency in 1893, Gray Gables served as his summer vacation headquarters. As a man who preferred his Bourne neighbors to call him "Grover" rather than "Mr. President," Cleveland fit in well with the locals.

An avid fisherman and outdoor sportsman, the President spent his leisure time among the ponds and forests of the Upper Cape and he appreciated the privacy that Cape Cod gave him. "I have only to behave myself and pay my taxes to be treated like any other citizen of the United States," he told a reporter from *Harper's Weekly*.

Following his second term of office, Cleveland and his family continued to frequent Gray Gables until the death of his oldest daughter Ruth in 1904. The memory of summer days spent at Gray Gables with his young family, and their connection to the loss of his first-born child, was so painful to the former President that the Clevelands never returned to their Cape Cod summer home again.

Provincetown became the scene of visits by Presidents Theodore Roosevelt and William Howard Taft during the building of the

Pilgrim Monument. In August of 1907, Roosevelt arrived in the presidential yacht *Mayflower* to dedicate the cornerstone of the building. Three years later, when the structure was complete, President Taft made the formal dedication of the memorial.

At a dinner in the town hall, Taft made reference to his Pilgrim ancestry and noted that he, like his ancestors, arrived at the Cape-tip in a vessel named *Mayflower*. It was pointed out by some that, unlike the Spartan conditions of the original Pilgrim ship, the presidential yacht reportedly had a specially designed bath tub to accommodate the large Chief Executive. Taft denied having such an extravagance saying "we have no special bath tubs made for any executive of any particular size."

Other than a short canal cruise by President Warren G. Harding in August of 1921 as he headed for a memorial celebration in Plymouth, and with the exception of President Kennedy, no sitting president arrived on Cape Cod until 1990. In the fall of that year George Bush landed at Otis Air Base in a campaign swing in support of Republican candidates in Massachusetts. Years before, during World War II, Bush was briefly stationed at the Hyannis airport as part of his training as a naval aviator.

Jutting into Atlantic, Cape Ideal for Rumrunners

In the 1920s, following the passage of the eighteenth amendment to the US Constitution, liquor was legally outlawed for all American citizens. The so-called "noble experiment" would have ramifications far beyond the original intent of this law that was supposed to dry up the country.

Entrepreneurs quickly seized upon the opportunity to supply a prohibited item to a consuming public that seemed to delight in flaunting the law. Rumrunning became big business along the New England coast and Cape Cod, with its geographic "arm" perfectly situated to intercept the clandestine cargoes of booze, became a prime bootlegging territory. Canadian and European ships laden with liquor would anchor twelve miles off the coast on what came to be known as "Rum Row."

The twelve-mile line was the end of Coast Guard jurisdiction and the bootleggers offered their supplies of bourbon, rye, champagne, scotch and cognac to passing vessels with impunity. Cape Cod fishermen would pull up to these ships and strike deals with the captains and then run the booze ashore on moonless or foggy nights.

With the Coast Guard stretched out over a large coastal patrol area, skillful captains could bring a cargo into a deserted cove and deliver it to waiting trucks. The profits were huge and a man could make as much as $400 a month in the illegal liquor trade.

Each town had individuals that were involved in liquor smuggling. Even a single successful liquor drop could pay the bills of a local fisherman for a good part of the year.

Perhaps the most celebrated rumrunner from the Cape was captain Manny Zora of Provincetown. Zora, a Portuguese fisherman who later became the subject of a book by Scott Corbett, was known as "The Sea Fox" because of his ability to slip through the Coast Guard patrols in his fishing vessel, the *Mary Ellen*.

In the dark of night or under the shroud of a spring fog, this colorful rogue delivered cases of contraband to thirsty consumers all along the length of Cape Cod.

Zora was something of a folk hero to the Portuguese community at the Cape-tip and his exploits were recounted for years after he quit the trade, reportedly as a wealthy man, retiring to spend his last days in his native Portugal.

Stealth and cunning marked the successful rumrunner and people like Zora found a ready market for the liquor that they transported.

Despite the laws and the coastal patrols, it wasn't difficult to obtain liquor during the height of Prohibition. Most towns featured "tea rooms" where a person could get a drink. "Speakeasies" and roadhouses proliferated during the 1920s to the point where locals winked at the activities that went on in them. The Casa Madrid in South Yarmouth was such a well-known Mid-Cape watering hole that it attracted a celebrity crowd that reportedly included some of Massachusetts' best known politicians.

Otherwise respectable citizens took the opportunity to profit from the liquor trade whenever possible. The lighthouse keeper in

Chatham was caught storing bootleg whiskey in the fog horn building. One Brewster selectman is reported to have made it a practice to store his water-dropped whiskey in a fish weir off Robbins Hill Beach.

A person who could be counted on to keep his mouth shut could make twenty-five or thirty dollars in a single night unloading cases of booze from a rumrunner. In the fragile economy that existed on Cape Cod in the 1920s and early 1930s, the temptations of the rumrunning trade were difficult to resist.

As romantic as many of the stories make it, there was still an element of violence connected with the whiskey trade. With potential profits so high, organized crime was naturally attracted to the bootlegging business. While most rumrunning encounters with the authorities, or even with hijackers, ended with perhaps a few bruised knuckles, a small fine, or the loss of the cargo, rumrunning could turn deadly.

In 1923, the Newport, Rhode Island based rumrunner *John Dwight* was apparently caught in a "turf war" over who had the rights to run booze into Martha's Vineyard. In this area's deadliest bootleg shoot-out, the *Dwight* was apparently sunk by a competitor and its crew of nine men were tortured and set adrift to die in the cold April sea. With no witnesses, it could only be surmised that the fate of the *Dwight* crew resulted because someone wanted to send a strong message that competitors were not welcome in Vineyard Sound.

But there was humor in the story of rumrunning as well. In December of 1922, the Canadian rumrunner *Annie Spindler* was driven by the winds of a northeaster onto the Provincetown beach near the Race Point Coast Guard station. She sailed from Nova Scotia with a large cargo of whiskey and it was pretty certain that if the unfortunate storm did not leave her on the sand, the *Spindler* would have sold her cargo from the safety of her Rum Row anchorage.

By a strange twist of fate, the Coast Guard was obligated to assist the captain in bringing his cargo of booze from the wrecked ship to another vessel that was tied up in Provincetown Harbor. As a foreign vessel, the *Spindler* and her cargo were eligible for protection because she carried papers indicating that her destination was the West Indies. The Coast Guard, faced with a simple act of God, had no choice but to assist in the transfer of the liquor. This was done, although at a considerable loss of much of the cargo at the hands of willing local "volunteers" who made off with a good deal of the merchandise.

What was left was loaded onto the second vessel and shortly after departing Provincetown under the cover of darkness the remainder of the booze was run into shore at a secluded cove further up Cape.

On another occasion, on a moonless night, a rumrunner was being chased by a Coast Guard cutter outside of Billingsgate shoal. As the searchlight began to probe his wake, the captain decided to drop his cargo overboard in shallow water, marking his position so as to be able to return later to pick it up.

During the next day, word of the drop spread through the local community and, to his dismay, when the rumrunner returned he found that several hundred Cape Codders were already in position dragging the bottom for the jettisoned whiskey. The activity of so many "fishermen" in one place eventually attracted the Coast Guard and by evening, most of the liquor was confiscated.

Although it hasn't happened recently, an occasional bottle of bootleg whiskey will still show up in the shifting tidal flats of Cape Cod Bay. In the early 1960s a Brewster sea clammer stumbled on several bottles still with the corks in them. The report that he shared with friends was that the taste of the booze wasn't compromised a bit by its lengthy sleep in the sand.

Chapter 8

Witches, Ghosts & Sea Serpents

On a peninsula settled nearly four centuries ago one is bound to encounter some ghosts, witches, sea serpents and even the Devil himself from time to time. It all adds up to legend and lore uniquely Cape Cod.

We conclude here with a few tales from Cape Cod's darker and more mysterious side, from eighteenth century witches Goody Hallett and Liza Tower Hill to nineteenth and twentieth century sea serpents discovered just off these outer shores!

The Tragedy of Goody Hallett

The discovery of the pirate ship *Whidah* has shed light into the activities of pirate Captain "Black Sam" Bellamy and his ill-fated band of buccaneers. The loss of the ship and most of her crew in the winter of 1717 produced a number of legends about buried gold, the sounds of death, and ghostly apparitions on foggy nights at the Cape's outer shore.

Josef Berger, who wrote the 1930's classic *Cape Cod Pilot*, told the story of the simple Eastham farm girl whose fate was linked with the wreck of the *Whidah*. Her name was "Goody" Hallett.

How good "Goody" Hallett was is a matter of some speculation. It seems that she made the acquaintance of Captain Bellamy when he visited Eastham some years before he and his ship were done in by a northeaster. While he stayed the warm months at the Crosby Tavern, Bellamy met and sweet-talked sixteen year old Maria Hallett. The handsome pirate's tales of wealth and adventure impressed the wide-eyed Cape lass and there was talk of love. He convinced her that he would return and marry her once he cleared up some business in the Caribbean. As September brought its chilly evenings, he sailed away without her.

Some months after his departure, Maria Hallett gave birth to a child that died the same night. The event caused such a scandal in the small town that the selectmen threw the poor girl in jail. While in prison she became so distraught that she lost her mind. Escaping frequently, she wandered the dunes of the Atlantic shore looking seaward for her lost lover. Eastham ceased its attempts to confine the girl and she was eventually cast out of town with the stipulation that she never return. She was reduced to scratching out a living doing menial jobs and lived in a lonely shack near the shore at South Wellfleet.

As years passed, Maria became a shell of her once beautiful self and residents began to refer to her as a witch who sold her soul to the Devil. They called her "Goody" and told stories of seeing her in the dunes on cold windy nights screaming curses into the storm on the head of Captain Sam Bellamy, the man who betrayed her.

As for Captain Bellamy, he had long forgotten Maria and his pleasant summer in Eastham. He developed quite a reputation for himself and, with his band of brigands, he terrorized ships in the Caribbean. But it may have been the memory of warm Eastham nights that caused him to bring his ship back to New England. Or perhaps it was because the price on his head was high enough for him to decide to seek plunder in different waters. At any rate, he arrived off the coast of Cape Cod in the winter of 1717 only to fall victim to a massive storm. Despite all the efforts of the crew, the *Whidah* struck the bar off South Wellfleet and went to pieces. As men screamed their last in the raging surf, people along the beach saw "Goody" Hallett standing on the high bluffs shrieking her thanks to the Devil for vengeance.

In the aftermath of the wreck, the story grew that "Goody" Hallett somehow managed to retrieve and conceal a chest of pirate gold from the ship. Because Sam Bellamy's body was never recovered it was also rumored that he escaped the sinking ship and was ashore in search of his lost treasure.

The legend developed that the buried gold is still somewhere in Wellfleet because "Goody" Hallett forgot where she buried it, taking the secret to her grave. For many years after the *Whidah* wreck, local residents reported picking up gold coins along the Atlantic beach after great storms.

Was there a buried treasure? No one really knows. Perhaps the secret did die with "Goody" Hallett and the remainder of the treasure lies waiting for someone to stumble on it.

Liza Tower Hill – Witch of Half Way Pond

The story of Elizabeth Lewis, later Elizabeth Blatchford, referred to by the local townsfolk as Liza Tower Hill - the Witch of Half Way Pond, is in reality two stories. There is the story of fact concerning the woman who raised a family in the wilderness of eighteenth century Barnstable and there is the folklore woven by the townsfolk, forever labeling the woman a witch.

Let us begin with the fact and then move to the popular folklore.

Elizabeth Lewis was born on January 17, 1711 to Benjamin Lewis of Barnstable and his second wife, Hannah Hinckley, also of Barnstable. Hannah was a cousin of Massachusetts Governor Thomas Hinckley. She died when Elizabeth was a child leaving Benjamin to raise his daughter alone at their home near Crooked Pond, now Lampson's Pond, in the wilderness between the villages of Barnstable to the north and Hyannis to the south. They lived two miles from their nearest neighbor.

From the very beginning Elizabeth Lewis was viewed as "odd"

by the townsfolk of neighboring Hyannis and Barnstable. She did not possess the feminine qualities of her contemporaries in the more populated areas and can best be described as a tomboy, one quite learned in farming and the ways of the forest.

At that time the wilderness was known to harbor Indians and wild animals, but to Elizabeth and her widowed father these Indians and animals were merely neighbors and not to be feared as long as they were treated with respect. The townsfolk, on the other hand, were not accustomed to such hostilities and therefore could not understand the Lewis' "strange" way of life.

At the age of seventeen, Elizabeth married William Blatchford on November 12, 1728. Blatchford built a home in the very same wilderness on Half Way Pond, now Mary Dunn Pond, one mile west of Benjamin Lewis' house. The trodden Indian trail that led from Barnstable to Hyannis, now known as Mary Dunn Road, ran right past the pond.

The Blatchfords had eight children, beginning with Peter in 1729 and ending with William in 1750. The second child, Lydia, died very young. The seventh child, born in 1746, was also named Lydia and worked as a servant at the Allyn House in Barnstable. That tale will be told later.

Admitted as a member of the East Church of Barnstable in January 1736/37, Elizabeth "was an exemplary member" with only one mishap to mar her otherwise spotless church record. It seems that when the first Lydia died, Thankful Gilbert, a member of the church, charged Elizabeth with abuse. As punishment, she was forced to read her confession of guilt aloud in public.

Her husband was not religious and did not accompany his wife to service. He himself was admitted as a member of the church only the day before his death, which occurred on June 15, 1755, leaving Elizabeth alone to raise her children.

In order to earn a living she spun, wove, cared for sick animals and farmed. She was hardworking and was described by Amos Otis in his book *Genealogical Notes of Barnstable Families* as "honest, industrious, energetic and shrewd in making a bargain."

The Barnstable town records of 1773 show her being fined for "selling spirituous liquor without a license." There is evidence of her performing hard physical labor into her seventy-fifth year of age. In June 1790 she died and was buried in the graveyard at the East Church where she was a member.

Since the townsfolk could not understand her way of life apart from the rest of the population, Elizabeth became a scapegoat and labeled a witch. Though she protested this label, the taunting and gossip and the tall tales followed her to her death, and beyond her death, in fact to this very day.

The townsfolk believed that she could not have survived in such a hostile forest setting without some form of assistance. In eighteenth century New England there was no understanding an independent woman forging her own life, maintaining a farm and raising children on her own. She clearly required outside help, supernatural help, and it was believed that such help came from the Devil himself.

She was dubbed by the townsfolk Liza Tower Hill, referring to the Tower Hill section of London whence her husband's ancestors hailed. At night, under the moon's glow, it was rumored that Liza performed a devil dance upon the surface of Half Way Pond, bare breasted and with her feet aglow. Devil fish would swim below her, aflame. Strange, mutant animals would appear on shore. Lights would shine in the forest as horses carrying riders from Barnstable to Hyannis would become bewitched by Liza Tower Hill's craft. Even after her death in 1790 it was believed that her ghost haunted the forest and the pond, bewitching those who dared travel the dark path by night.

There exist a number of stories concerning Elizabeth Blatchford's alter ego Liza Tower Hill, folklore, stories of her as both a witch and a ghost.

A Mr. Wood of West Barnstable brought a formal charge against Elizabeth Blatchford, the only one on record, accusing her of being a witch. He claimed she would turn him into a horse and ride him to Plum Pudding Pond in Plymouth in order to attend Witches' Sabbaths and to participate in satanic orgies. Wood's case was dropped for lack of evidence.

Benjamin Goodspeed of East Sandwich also claimed that the witch Liza Tower Hill would turn him into a horse and ride him all night long over Cape Cod. In an effort to escape these nocturnal bewitchings Goodspeed went to sea, figuring he was safe on board a sailing vessel far from the bewitched forest of Barnstable, but the witch chased him in the form of her familiar, a black cat.

One evening, according to folklore, a black cat swam up to the ship, boarded the vessel and then transformed itself into Liza Tower Hill. The witch then turned Goodspeed into a horse and rode him throughout the night. The next evening, presumably one night in June 1790, the cat again swam after the vessel, but this time Goodspeed was ready. On the advice of a shipmate, using a wet page from the Bible rolled into a pellet, he aimed his rifle and shot dead the swimming cat. At that same moment, Liza Tower Hill, upon the death of her familiar, also died in her hut in the forest.

After her death it was believed that the witch's ghost haunted two places in the town of Barnstable – the forest wilderness where she had lived and the Allyn House in Barnstable.

On Christmas night 1810, seventy-one-year-old Dr. Richard Bourne was headed home along the old Indian trail after celebrating at a local pub. As he neared the area of Half Way Pond he noticed what appeared to be a burning stump around which danced the ghost of Liza Tower Hill. Bourne, in a fit of holiday merriment it would seem, spent the night singing and dancing around the stump with the ghost. Come the next morning he awoke alone, and presumably with a hangover.

The Allyn House was believed haunted by the ghost of Liza Tower Hill. Even before her death, her familiar, a black cat, was believed to haunt the house in revenge for the apparent mistreatment of her daughter Lydia by the employers at this house where she worked as a servant. The Allyns were a wealthy and well-respected Barnstable family, as respected as the Hinckley family to which Elizabeth Blatchford and her daughter Lydia could claim lineage.

Built in 1680, the Allyn House is believed today to be among the oldest houses on Cape Cod. Soon after Lydia was hired on at the house strange things began to happen, things to be blamed upon the witch Liza Tower Hill, and after her death, upon her ghost.

First the Allyn children came down with fevers. Then fresh milk turned sour, supposedly a sign of demonic forces at work. Clocks and dishes would suddenly be smashed, sometimes in the middle of the night.

The family was kept awake at night by knocks upon the walls and other unholy sounds. Six chairs, which were purchased just the day before, were found smashed to bits by invisible hands. And a black cat strangely made its appearance whenever the servant Lydia was either mistreated or made to do more work than her mother felt she should do.

Of course, these stories of familiars and ghosts and turning men into horses are folktales that have survived more than two hundred years, and will perhaps survive another two hundred.

But let us remember also that behind the folklore is the true story of a woman, not a witch, who grew up in the wilderness of eighteenth century Barnstable. She married, raised children, died and was buried as a member of the church, in the soil of the town where she made her home.

Sea Serpents Over the Centuries

Sea serpents have long been a part of Cape Cod history since Henry Hudson first sighted a mermaid on a Cape beach back in 1609.

The Native Indians of Martha's Vineyard had their own sea serpent stories, including the tale of the sea woman named Squant with hair of green seaweed, a body of kelp and eyes shaped of squares. She lived in an underwater cave off Aquinnah where the giant Indian spirit Maushop lay asleep, enchanted by the sea woman's song that led him from the dry land to her watery den.

A little more than one hundred years after Henry Hudson sighted his mermaid, Benjamin Franklin's uncle saw a serpent off Cape Cod in September 1719. It was sixteen feet long and had a head like a lion, large teeth, a long beard and floppy ears like those of an elephant. A boat crew took chase and actually harpooned the beast. For five hours they hunted the serpent until finally it disappeared beneath the waves.

In October 1817, the Linnaen Society of Boston formed a committee to gather evidence on a sea serpent that apparently pestered fishermen in Cape Cod waters. Due to lack of evidence, the committee was eventually dissolved.

Sixteen years later, in 1833, reports abounded of a large snake-like serpent in Massachusetts Bay. Word came down from Boston that the city would pay to have this serpent hunted down and killed. The whaling men of Nantucket answered the call. Out of the old whaling port came the sloop *Fame* carrying a crew of skilled whalers and all the tools of the trade necessary to hunt down the leviathan.

For two solid weeks they cruised the waters of Cape Cod and Massachusetts bays, but no sea serpent was found. The bored crew grew restless, prompting four crew members to desert. Dejected, they sailed back to Nantucket without casting a harpoon.

The next reported sighting on Cape Cod is perhaps her most famous, as the account was published in newspapers across the country. The year was 1886. Provincetown town crier George Washington Ready, nicknamed "The Professor," was walking the beach down at Herring Cove when he noticed an angry commotion offshore. Water was sprayed some fifty feet in the air. Ready hid behind a bush and witnessed a massive sea serpent coming ashore.

The beast was about three hundred feet long and twelve feet wide. Its body was covered with alternating green, blue and red scales. Upon its head, a head described as the size of a two hundred gallon cask - convex on top and concave on the bottom - were six eyes "as large as dinner plates." Three eyes were red, the other three were green. The mouth possessed four rows of two-foot long teeth. Ready said that the head, which was crowned with an eight-foot horn, rested some thirty feet in the air.

A sulfuric odor came from the beast as it passed and some inner heat radiated from its scales, burning bushes that it touched. The beast was followed by a twenty-foot tail.

Ready watched as the serpent made its way to Pasture Pond where it disappeared from sight down a bottomless chasm in the pond's center. A friend of Ready's, who penned an article documenting what he saw, believed that perhaps recent earthquakes awoke the sea serpent from its underwater slumber. Ready concluded his statement by saying that at the time he witnessed this strange event he was "not *unduly* excited by liquor or otherwise."

In January 1936, an Orleans Coast Guardsman sighted what he thought were sea serpents possessing tongues like fish tails and mouths holding two hundred teeth. He claimed that while walking the beach he also discovered a carcass of one of these beasts washed up on shore. Experts brought in to examine the serpent carcass quickly determined it to be that of a dolphin and could only conclude that the beasts the Coast Guardsman saw swimming offshore were the same.

Aquinnah (Gay Head) has been the site of a number of sea serpent sightings over the centuries, from the account of an officer on board a British vessel just prior to the Revolutionary War to a more recent sighting in March 1940. Thoughts of Squant the sea woman in her watery cavern come to mind with the reports of leviathans sighted in the Aquinnah Cliffs area.

The crew of a Fairhaven fishing boat sighted a beast near Menemsha Creek. It had claw-like flippers that reached out and pushed aside their vessel, and possessed a head resembling that of a cow. The serpent's head had eyes the size of dinner plates, sounding very much like the description given by George Washington Ready of the nineteenth century serpent that came ashore at Provincetown.

The crew of a fishing boat also made the March 1940 sighting, this time off Nomans Land. They described a fifty-foot serpent with a lizard-like body and the head of a turtle. The beast had flippers and a long tail with a triangular tip. It "looked like something very old" reported the captain of the fishing vessel in an attempt to describe the oddity he apparently saw.

Being thrust as it is some forty miles out into the raging sea, Cape Cod is bound to have its share of sea serpents. The oceans beyond the continental shelf drop off to unimaginable depths. We have only just begun to map what lies beneath the waves. Who knows what strange and wondrous things are yet to be discovered.

Fishermen occasionally snag some unknown creature in their

nets that baffles even the scientists, sometimes netting creatures thought extinct tens of thousands or even millions of years ago. Who knows what creatures swim through the depths where even the sun's light cannot penetrate ... creatures, one would imagine, with large eyes "the size of dinner plates" in order to capture what little light does exist at such depths.

And who can say for sure what creatures have come forth from these depths to visit the waters off Cape Cod!

What strange beasts lurk in the waters off the Cape's outermost shores? (J. Sheedy photo)

BIBLIOGRAPHY

Barbour, Harriot Buxton. Sandwich - The Town That Glass Built. Boston, MA: Houghton Mifflin Co., 1948.

Barnstable County. Three Centuries of a Cape Cod County: Barnstable, Massachusetts, 1685-1985. Barnstable, MA: Barnstable County, 1985.

Benton, Josiah H. Warning Out in New England. Boston, MA: W.B. Clark Co., 1911.

Beston, Henry. The Outermost House. Garden City, NY: Doubleday, Doran & Co, Inc, 1929.

Bingham, Amelia. Mashpee: Land of the Wampanoags. Mashpee, MA: Mashpee Centennial Committee, 1970.

Bradford, William. Bradford's History of Plymouth Plantation. Boston, MA: Wright & Potter Printing Co, 1898.

Bray, Mary Mathews. A Sea Trip in Clipper Ship Days. Boston, MA: Badger, 1920

Brigham, Albert Perry. Cape Cod and the Old Colony. New York, NY: Grosset & Dunlap, 1920.

Burrows, Fredrika A. Cannonballs & Cranberries. Taunton, MA: Wm. S. Sullwold Publishing, Inc., 1976.

Burrows, Fredrika A. Windmills on Cape Cod and the Islands. Taunton, MA: Wm. S. Sullwold Publishing, Inc., 1978.

Cabral, Reginald W. Wooden Ships and Iron Men. Provincetown, MA: Trustees of the Provincetown Heritage Museum, 1994.

Carpenter, Edmund J., The Pilgrims and Their Monument. New York, NY: D. Appleton and Co., 1911.

Cataldo, Louis. Pictorial Tales of Cape Cod. Hyannis, MA: Tales of Cape Cod, Inc, 1956.

Chatham, Dennis & Marion. Cape Coddities. Boston, MA & New York, NY: Houghton Mifflin Co, 1920.

Clark, Admont G. Lighthouses of Cape Cod, Martha's Vineyard, Nantucket. East Orleans, MA: Parnassus Imprint, 1992.

Clark, Admont G. They Built Clipper Ships in Their Back Yard. Yarmouthport, MA: Parnassus Imprint, 1963.

Corbett, Scott. The Sea Fox. New York, NY: Thomas Y. Crowell Company, 1956.

Corbett, Scott. We Chose Cape Cod. New York, NY: Thomas Y. Crowell Co, 1953.

Crosby, Katharine. Blue-Water Men & Other Cape Codders. New York, NY: The Macmillan Company, 1946.

Cullity, Rosanna and John Nye. A Sandwich Album. Sandwich, MA: Nye Family of America Society, 1987.

Dalton, J.W. The Lifesavers of Cape Cod. Chatham, MA: The Chatham Press, Inc., 1967.

Darling, Edward. Three Old Timers of Cape Cod. Hyannis, MA: Wake-Brook House, 1974.

Davis, William T. Plymouth Memories of an Octogenarian. Plymouth, MA: The Memorial Press, 1906.

Depauw, Linda Grant. Seafaring Women. Boston, MA: Houghton-Mifflin Co., 1982.

Deyo, Simeon L. History of Barnstable County, Massachusetts 1620-1890. New York, NY: H.W. Blake & Co, 1890.

Digges, Jeremiah (Josef Berger). Cape Cod Pilot. Provincetown, MA & New York, NY: Modern Pilgrim Press and Viking Press, 1937.

Doane, Doris. Exploring Old Cape Cod. Chatham, MA: The Chatham Press, Inc., 1968.

Early, Eleanor. Cape Cod Summer. Boston, MA: Houghton-Mifflin Co., 1936.

Eastham Tercentenary Committee. Eastham Massachusetts, 1651-1951. Eastham, MA: Eastham Tercentenary Committee, 1951.

Echeverria, Donald. A History of Billingsgate. Wellfleet, MA: Wellfleet Historical Society, 1991.

Fawsett, Marise. Cape Cod Annals. Bowie, MD: Heritage Books, Inc., 1990.

Farson, Robert. Cape Cod Railroads: Including Martha's Vineyard and Nantucket. Yarmouth Port, MA: Cape Cod Historical Publications, 1990.

Freeman, Frederick. The History of Cape Cod. Yarmouth Port, MA: Parnassus Imprints, 1965.

Frost, Jack. A Cape Cod Sketchbook. New York, NY: Coward-McCann, Inc, 1939.

Giambarba, Paul. Surfmen and Lifesavers. Centerville, MA: Scrimshaw Publishing, 1967.

Giambarba, Paul. The Picture Story of Cape Cod. Centerville, MA: The Scrimshaw Press: 1965.

Gibson, Marjorie Hubbell. Historical & Genealogical Atlas and Guide to Barnstable County. Teaticket, MA: Falmouth Genealogical Society, 1995.

Green, Eugene and William Sachse. Names of the Land. Chester, CT: Globe Pequot Press, 1983.

Holly, H.H. Sparrow-hawk: A Seventeenth Century Vessel in Twentieth Century America. Boston, MA: The Nimrod Press, 1969.

Jalbert, Russell R. 4000 Years of Life in Orleans. Orleans, MA: Orleans Bicentennial Commission, 1997.

Janes, Edward C. When Cape Cod Men Saved Lives. Champaign, IL: Garrard Publishing Co., 1968.

Johnson, Jack. Stories of Cape Cod. Plymouth, MA: Memorial Press of Plymouth, 1944.

Kane, Tom. My Pamet. Mount Kisco, NY: Moyer Bell Limited, 1989.

Keene, Betsey D. History of Bourne from 1622 to 1937. Yarmouthport, MA: Charles W. Swift, 1937.

Kittredge, Henry C. Cape Cod: Its People & Their History. Boston, MA: Houghton Mifflin Company, 1968.

Kittredge, Henry C. Mooncussers of Cape Cod. New York, NY: Houghton Mifflin Co., 1937.

Kittredge, Henry C. Shipmasters of Cape Cod. Boston, MA & New York, NY: Houghton Mifflin Company, 1935.

Knowles, Katharine. Cape Cod Journey. Barre, MA: Barre Publishers, 1966.

Lawson, Evelyn. Yesterday's Cape Cod. Miami, FL: E.A. Seemann Publishing, Inc., 1975.

Leighton, Clare. Where Land Meets Sea. Chatham, MA: The Chatham Press, Inc., 1973.

Lincoln, Joseph C. Cape Cod Yesterdays. New York, NY: Blue Ribbon Books, 1939.

Lombard Jr., Asa Cobb Paine. East of Cape Cod. New Bedford, MA: Reynolds-De Walt Printing, Inc, 1976.

Lowe, Alice A. Nauset on Cape Cod - A History of Eastham. Eastham, MA: Eastham Historical Society, 1968.

Neal, Allan. Cape Cod is a Number of Things. Yarmouth Port, MA: The Register Press, 1954.

Noble, Frederick A. The Pilgrims. Cambridge, MA: The University Press, 1907.

Oldale, Robert N. Cape Cod and the Islands: The Geologic Story. East Orleans, MA: Parnassus Imprint, 1992.

Orleans Historical Society. Rescue CG36500. Orleans, MA: Lower Cape Publishing, 1985.

Otis, Amos. Genealogical Notes of Barnstable Families. Barnstable, MA: F.B. & F.P. Goss Publishers and Printers, 1888.

Pohl, Frederick J. The Vikings on Cape Cod. Pictou, Nova Scotia: Pictou Advocate Press, 1957.

Quinn, William P. Shipwrecks Around Cape Cod. Orleans, MA: Lower Cape Publishing, 1973.

Quinn, William P. The Saltworks of Historic Cape Cod. Orleans, MA: Parnassus Imprint, 1993.

Reynard, Elizabeth. The Narrow Land. Chatham, MA: Chatham Historical Society, 1978.

Rex, Percy Fielitz. The Prolific Pencil: A Biography of Joseph Crosby Lincoln. Taunton, MA: William S. Sullwold Publishing, Inc., 1980.

Ryder, Marion Crowell. Cape Cod Remembrances. Taunton, MA: William S. Sullwold Publishing, 1972.

Schwind, Phil. Making a Living Alongshore. Camden, ME: International Marine Publishing Co, 1976.

Small, Isaac M. Shipwrecks on Cape Cod. Chatham, MA: The Chatham Press, Inc., 1967.

Smith, Mary Lou. The Book of Falmouth: A Tercentennial Celebration 1686-1986. Falmouth, MA: Falmouth Historical Society, 1986.

Smith, Mary Lou. Woods Hole Reflections. Woods Hole, MA: Woods Hole Historical Society, 1983.

Smith, William C. A History of Chatham, Massachusetts. Chatham, MA: Chatham Historical Society, 1971.

Snow, Edward Rowe. A Pilgrim Returns to Cape Cod. Boston, MA: The Yankee Publishing Co., 1946.

Snow, Edward Rowe. New England Sea Tragedies: New York, NY: Dodd, Mead & Co., 1960.

Snow, Edward Rowe. The Lighthouses of New England. New York, NY: Dodd, Mead & Co., 1945

Sprague, Mary A. A Cape Cod Village. Hyannis, MA: The Patriot Press, 1963.

Swift, Charles F. Cape Cod. Yarmouthport, MA: Register Publishing Company, 1897.

Swift, Charles F. History of Old Yarmouth. Yarmouthport, MA: The Historical Society of Old Yarmouth, 1975.

Tarbell, Arthur Wilson. Cape Cod Ahoy. Boston, MA: A.T. Ramsay and Co, 1932.

Thomas, Joseph D. Cranberry Harvest. New Bedford, MA: Spinner Publications, Inc., 1990.

Thompson, Frederic L. The Lightships of Cape Cod. Portland, ME: Congress Square Press, 1983.

Thoreau, Henry David. Cape Cod. New York, NY: Bramhall House, 1951.

Town of Barnstable. The Seven Villages of Barnstable. Barnstable, MA: Town of Barnstable, 1976.

Trayser, Donald G. Barnstable: Three Centuries of a Cape Cod Town. Hyannis, MA: F.B. & F.P. Goss, 1939.

Vuilleumier, Marion. Cape Cod - A Pictorial History. Norfolk, VA: The Donning Co., 1982.

Vuilleumier, Marion. Earning a Living on Olde Cape Cod. Craigville, MA: Craigville Press, 1968.

Vuilleumier, Marion. Sketches of Old Cape Cod. Taunton, MA: Wm. S. Sullwold Publishing, 1972.

Vuilleumier, Marion. The Town of Yarmouth, Massachusetts - A History: 1639-1989. Yarmouth, MA: The Historical Society of Old Yarmouth, 1989.

Waldron, Nan Turner. Journey to Outermost House. Bethlehem, CT: Butterfly & Wheel Publishing, 1991.

Webber, Bernard C. Chatham "The Lifeboatmen." Orleans, MA. Lower Cape Publishing Co., 1985.

Whiting, Emma Mayhew & Henry Beetle Hough. Whaling Wives. Boston, MA: Houghton-Mifflin Co., 1953.

Wood, Donald. Cape Cod - A Guide. Boston, MA: Little, Brown & Co., 1973.
Barnstable Patriot, "The Family Physicians of the Yesterdays of Hyannis," by Clara J. Hallett.
Barnstable Patriot, February 12, 1899.
Barnstable Patriot, July/August 1897.
Boston Globe, "Bodies Told Tale of Torture at Sea," by David Arnold, July 31, 1996.
Boston Globe, by Donald B. Willard, July/August, 1928.
Cape Cod and all the Pilgrim Land, "Cape Cod Pearls," May 1921.
Cape Cod Compass, "The Cape's Two Summer White Houses," by Marion Vuilleumier, Vol. 30, 1982.
Cape Cod Life, "Turn of the Century Vacations," by Cliff Henderson, June/July 1990.
Cape Cod Life, "Seafaring Women of the 19th Century: Their Encounters with Pirates, Storms and Mutiny," by James and Mary Coogan, Early Summer 1986.
Cape Cod Mariner: The Journal of the Kittredge Maritime Center, "Native Pearls from herring streams," by James Coogan, Spring 1994.
Cape Cod Times, "His Branded Hand was Abolitionists' Call to Arms," by James Coogan, January 16, 1983.
Falmouth Enterprise, May 19, 1961.
Falmouth Enterprise, "Life at Gray Gables was Unostentatious for Ex-President," May 25, 1990.
Provincetown Advocate, March 14, 1878.
The Cape, by Robert P. Ashley, June, 1967.
The Register, November 21, 1952.
The Register, by Barbara Macphee, July 21, 1977.

Research was also gathered at: Barnstable Vital records; Mashpee Archives/Vital Records; Old Dartmouth Historical Society; Pilgrim Hall Museum; Sandwich Historical Society; Sturgis Library and William Brewster Nickerson Room - Cape Cod Community College.

Notes from Chapter 2:
Sources for "The Colonial Custom of Warning Out" essay included: Cape Cod by Charles F. Swift, 1897; Cape Cod: Its People and Their History by Henry C. Kittredge, 1968; and Warning Out in New England: 1656-1817 by Josiah H. Benton, 1911.

Notes from Chapter 7:
1 Logbook of the New Bedford whaler Gazelle, 1857; Old Dartmouth Historical Society.
2 Whaling Wives by Emma Mahew Whiting and Henry Beetle Hough, 1953, page 7.
3 A Sea Trip in Clipper Ship Days by Mary Mathews Bray, 1920.
4 A Sea Trip in Clipper Ship Days by Mary Mathews Bray, 1920.
5 Logbook of the brig Panama, March 28, 1854; Pilgrim Memorial Museum.
6 Register, November 21, 1952, page 6.
7 Logbook of the brig Panama, March 28, 1854; Pilgrim Memorial Museum.
8 Hannah Rebecca Crowell Burgess Journals, 1852-1856; Sandwich Historical Society
9 My Pamet by Tom Kane, 1989; page 252.

ABOUT THE AUTHORS

Jim Coogan was raised on Cape Cod and grew up in the town of Brewster. Recently retired, he was a history teacher at Dennis-Yarmouth Regional High School for twenty-seven years. Cape Cod history is his special interest area and he is a popular lecturer and writer on the subject. A contributor to *The Barnstable Patriot*'s history magazine *Summerscape* for the past seven years, he also writes for other Cape Cod newspapers and penned one of the history chapters for the book *Three Centuries of a Cape Cod County: Barnstable, Massachusetts 1685-1985*, published in the county's tercentennial year. Mr. Coogan lives in Dennis with his wife, Beth and their very spoiled Great Dane, Sussannah.

Jack Sheedy has been freelancing for *The Barnstable Patriot* since 1985 and has been contributing to *Summerscape* since 1989. He began writing while attending Stonehill College in North Easton, Massachusetts. Over the past decade and a half he has published more than 250 articles and short stories and has authored three other books: *Dennis Journal, Autumn Cape Cod*, and *The Insider's Guide to Cape Cod, Nantucket & Martha's Vineyard* (second edition co-author). He is currently at work on a collection of short stories entitled *Phantom Fleet and Other Cape Cod Ghost Stories*. Jack lives in East Dennis with his wife Adriana, their children Gregory and Melissa, and their Boston Terrier, Lucy.

ABOUT THE BARNSTABLE PATRIOT

The Barnstable Patriot, founded in 1830 by Major Sylvanus Bourne Phinney, is published weekly in Hyannis and remains the third oldest continuously operating newspaper in New England. It charts the activities, large and less so, of the town of Barnstable's seven villages and records the events which comprise the town's life, both public and private. *The Patriot* engages the issues of the day in town and on Cape fully cognizant of the past and fiercely hopeful of the future. Samples of *The Patriot*'s weekly fare can be found at their web site, www.barnstablepatriot.com

ACKNOWLEDGMENTS

I would like to express particular gratitude to Mary Sicchio, Special Collections Librarian for the William Brewster Nickerson Room at Cape Cod Community College. Her knowledge of the collection and her willingness to assist my research was invaluable. My interest in history has also been supported by my family. My children endured countless vacation trips to historical sites when I'm sure they would have preferred visiting amusement parks. I thank them for humoring me and accepting my passion for history. Finally, nothing can ever be accomplished without the encouragement and understanding of a loving partner. My wife, Beth, put herself second on many occasions where history in one form or another took me away from things that I should have been doing around the house. Hers was a special support that made my efforts in this collection of essays possible.

Jim Coogan

My most sincere thanks to Toni and Rob Sennott, publishers of *The Barnstable Patriot*, for their complete support of *Cape Cod Companion* over these past three years and to David Still II for his editorial guidance and expertise. Responsible for the design of the text pages and the attractive cover is *Patriot* graphic artist Kristen vonHentschel who put in long hours and always with a smile on her face! My thanks to Dick Vecchione of J&D Advertising of Hyannis for his work on transferring the photos from Jim Coogan's collection to disk and to my wife, Adriana, for snapping the photo for the back cover – and for her years of support along the way. My children, Melissa and Gregory, also deserve a big thank you for accompanying me to many of the historical sites. Finally, thank you to those from centuries ago for creating the history that warrants our remembrance.

Jack Sheedy

The front cover image, from the Jim Coogan Collection, is entitled "An Old Salt" from a circa 1920s postcard printed by the C.T. American Art Colored Co., Chicago, IL. The back cover photograph is by Adriana Sheedy. Jim Coogan's postcard of the Nobscussett Hotel, on page 55, was originally published by E. C. Matthews & Co., Dennis, MA. The illustration of "the last moments of the steamer *Portland*" on page 105 is by John Thompson, 1990. Bishop & Clerks' lighthouse, on page 127, comes from a 1907 postcard to which the publisher added color and a light beam (from the Jim Coogan Collection). Special thanks to the Cape Cod National Seashore for allowing us to take photographs inside the Old Harbor lifesaving station that appear on pages 131 and 133.